"In addition to offering much-needed insight into sentencing policy and practice in post-communist Europe, this volume makes an important contribution to promoting better sentence justification. The chapters will be of interest to scholars and practitioners around the world."

—**Professor Julian V. Roberts, K.C. (Hon.)**, *Oxford University*

"This book provides the most valuable contribution to the discussion of judicial justifications of sentences in terms of the diagnosis of its nature, and proposals regarding proper approach to solving it."

—**Professor Krzysztof Krajewski**, *Jagiellonian University in Kraków*

Justifying Punishment

This book develops the principles of proper sentence justification, presents results of comparative empirical study on sentence justifications in the post-communist countries and provides practical measures to improve the current situation. Providing justification for sentences is an essential feature of any sentencing system that strives to achieve principled practice. Principled sentencing requires factors to be considered as well as explained both individually and comprehensively, in a manner that allows the process of determining the sentence to be reviewed and repeated with a similar result. This work determines why reasoning is relevant and provides compelling evidence in favour of an increased role for justification of sentences, grounded in the best sentencing, legal and psychological scholarship. It further explores how various theoretical and practical obstacles might be overcome. Relatedly, it introduces and expands on Schuyt's novel concept of justifying sentences, which approaches sentence justification in three stages. The authors investigate to what extent these stages are followed in practice in the Czech Republic, Estonia, Moldavia, Slovakia and Slovenia. The results suggest that the quality of sentence justification in these countries is generally low, although there is some variation. The book concludes with suggestions for improving the process and quality of sentence justification. The work will be of interest to those working in the areas of Criminal Law, Criminology, Comparative Law and Legal Philosophy.

Jakub Drápal is a researcher at the Institute of State and Law of the Czech Academy of Sciences, Czechia; an assistant professor at the Faculty of Law, Charles University, Czechia; and a MSCA-CZ fellow at Leiden University, the Netherlands.

Routledge Contemporary Issues in Criminal Justice and Procedure

Series Editor Ed Johnston is an Associate Professor of Criminal Justice and Procedure at the University of Northampton, UK.

Covid-19 and Criminal Justice
Impact and Legacy in England and Wales
Edited by Ed Johnston

Witness Protection and Criminal Justice in Africa
Nigeria in International Perspective
Suzzie Onyeka Oyakhire

Autism and Criminal Justice
The Experience of Suspects, Defendants and Offenders in England and Wales
Edited by Tom Smith

Robotics, AI and Criminal Law
Crimes against Robots
Kamil Mamak

Social Rehabilitation and Criminal Justice
Edited by Federica Coppola and Adriano Martufi

Neurolaw in the Courtroom
Comparative Perspectives on Vulnerable Defendants
Edited by Hannah Wishart and Colleen M. Berryessa

Contemporary Challenges in the Jury System
A Comparative Perspective
Nicola Monaghan

Implementation of Rights for Crime Victims in Theory and Practice
Lessons from India
Anupama Sharma

Justifying Punishment
Perspectives from Post-Communist Europe
Edited by Jakub Drápal

See more at https://www.routledge.com/Routledge-Research-in-Legal-History/book-series/CONTEMPCJP

Justifying Punishment

Perspectives from Post-Communist Europe

Edited by Jakub Drápal

Routledge
Taylor & Francis Group
LONDON AND NEW YORK

First published 2025
by Routledge
4 Park Square, Milton Park, Abingdon, Oxon OX14 4RN

and by Routledge
605 Third Avenue, New York, NY 10158

Routledge is an imprint of the Taylor & Francis Group, an informa business

British Library Cataloguing-in-Publication Data
A catalogue record for this book is available from the British Library

Library of Congress Cataloging-in-Publication Data
Names: Drápal, Jakub, editor.
Title: Justifying punishment: perspectives from post-Communist Europe / edited by Jakub Drápal.
Description: Abingdon, Oxon [UK]; New York, NY: Routledge, 2025. | Series: Routledge contemporary issues in criminal justice and procedure | Includes bibliographical references and index.
Identifiers: LCCN 2024041167 (print) | LCCN 2024041168 (ebook) | Subjects: LCSH: Punishment–Europe, Eastern. | Punishment–Europe, Central.. | Sentence (Criminal procedure)–Europe, Eastern. | Sentence (Criminal procedure)–Europe, Central. | Criminal justice, Administration of–Europe, Eastern. | Criminal justice, Administration of–Europe, Central.
Classification: LCC KJC8230 .J87 2025 (print) | LCC KJC8230 (ebook) | DDC 345.43/0773–dc23/eng/20240905
LC record available at https://lccn.loc.gov/2024041167
LC ebook record available at https://lccn.loc.gov/2024041168

ISBN: 978-1-032-72264-1 (hbk)
ISBN: 978-1-032-74744-6 (pbk)
ISBN: 978-1-003-47067-0 (ebk)

DOI: 10.4324/9781003470670

Typeset in Times New Roman
by Deanta Global Publishing Services, Chennai, India

Contents

Contributors

Augustina Bolocan-Holban is an associate professor at the State University of Moldova focusing on criminal law, comparative criminal law and probation. She is the director of the Association for Participatory Criminal Justice, a non-governmental organisation, which promotes alternatives to detention and restorative justice elements.

Jakub Drápal is a researcher at the Institute of State and Law of the Czech Academy of Sciences, Czechia; an assistant professor at the Faculty of Law, Charles University, Czechia; and a MSCA-CZ fellow at Leiden University, the Netherlands. He studies sentencing and penal policies using quantitative, comparative and doctrinal perspectives, focusing especially on continental and post-communist Europe.

Jaan Ginter is a professor of criminal law and criminology at the University of Tartuu. He focuses on studying sanctions, financial crime and the criminal justice system in general.

Sonja Meijer is a professor of penitentiary law at the Radboud University and an associate professor at the VU University Amsterdam focusing on criminal (procedural) law. She focuses on sanctions, penology and criminal procedure in a broad sense.

Mojca Plesničar is a senior research associate at the Institute of Criminology and associate professor of criminology at the University of Ljubljana. Her research focuses on sentencing and decision-making, emphasising a systemic approach, which involves recognizing patterns, interconnections, and the impacts of structures on judicial decision-making.

Pauline Schuyt is the president and director of the Dutch Academy for Legislation and Government Lawyers and a professor of penal law and sentencing at the Institute for Criminal Law and Criminology of Leiden University, the Netherlands. She is one of the leading experts on sentencing in the Netherlands.

Kristýna Tomšů is a civil servant at the Czech Office of the Government. She worked as a research assistant at the Institute of State and Law of the Czech Academy of Sciences, Czechia.

Tomáš Vanča is a PhD student at the Faculty of Law, Charles University, Czechia, and a law clerk. He was a research assistant at the Institute of State and Law of the Czech Academy of Sciences, Czechia.

Mihaela Vidaicu is an associate professor at the State University of Moldova. She is the country director of the ABA Rule of Law Initiative and was one those who introduced sentencing guidelines in Moldova. She publishes regularly on sentencing in Moldova.

Foreword

Julian V. Roberts

Our understanding of judicial decision-making at sentencing has grown immeasurably in recent decades. Better and more comprehensive court data, increased access to sentencers and more sophisticated analytic tools have all increased knowledge in this critical area of scholarship. However, most of the literature published in English has been very Anglo-centric. Much of this scholarship has focused on North America and Western Europe. One explanation for this geopolitical imbalance is that sentencing guidelines first emerged in the United States. Once these structures appeared, sentencing commissions and government agencies needed to better understand judicial reaction to the new structures. This stimulated research and commentary in guidelines jurisdictions. Despite their proliferation – around 40 jurisdictions now operate some form of guidelines – courts in the majority of civil and common-law countries still benefit from wide discretion.

Countries in Eastern Europe, and in particular those emerging from the ashes of the Soviet Union, have to date been overlooked in the English language literature. The current collection of essays by leading scholars is therefore a most welcome addition. More than that, it will prove to be a landmark volume, bringing the experience in these countries to the attention of scholars and practitioners around the world. Many of the problems of sentencing, including a lack of proportionality and sentencing disparity, exist in all sentencing systems. Accordingly, the experience confronting these problems in one jurisdiction may well have lessons for many others. Sentencing scholars in the Anglo-sphere may have much to learn from the experience in continental systems; learning is a two-way street.

The current volume is much more than a collection of country-based case histories. The contributors address a set of key questions which lie at the heart of the sentencing exercise. Central to their concerns is the issue of justifying legal punishment. Courts should always provide reasons and justifications for the sentences they impose on offenders. Fundamental justice requires that the reasons for any court-ordered liberty restriction be made clear, not just for the offender but also the crime victim and the wider community. As Dr Drápal notes in his introduction, providing a detailed justification for any sentence is "essential" for any sentencing regime which claims to be legitimate. Unfortunately, courts around the world sometime fall short of providing reasons and justifications to an acceptable standard. In addition to offering the much-needed insight into sentencing policy and practice in post-communist Europe, this volume therefore also makes an important contribution to promoting better sentence justification. The chapters will be of interest to scholars and practitioners around the world.

Julian V. Roberts, K.C. (Hon.)
University of Oxford

Acknowledgments

We are grateful to Jana Drápalová, Ondřej Kubů, Martin Lýsek, Julian Roberts, Kateřina Šimáčková, Hana Šimánová, Ondřej Šťastný, Jan Vychyta, Alena McClure and anonymous reviewers for comments on these and previous manuscripts. We are additionally thankful to Anna Magdalena Bartoň and Jonathan Edward Griffiths for proofreading the book, Lora Briški for assistance regarding Slovenian context and help with analysing Slovenian decisions, courts' administration and Jana Synková for providing and gathering court decisions and Wolters Kluwer CZ for their generous willingness to base some of the chapters on previously published articles in Czech (Drápal, 2019, 2020b, 2020a, 2023a; Vanča & Drápal, 2023).

Preparation of this book was funded by the Czech Grant Agency, project no. 19-15077S, titled "Sentencing disparities in the post-communist continental legal systems," carried out at the Institute of State and Law of the Czech Academy of Sciences. We are grateful for its support.

1 Introduction

Jakub Drápal

The most important feature of sentencing is discretion. For this reason, sentencing is governed by principles and not by rules, and as such it requires a different form of justification compared to the typical legal decision, in which a court has to "simply" argue whether one rule should apply or not. The sentence, on the contrary, is determined by the interaction of different principles that play varying roles depending on the context and that may result in a myriad of different outcomes. Given there is no gold standard – no single "right" sentence – in sentencing, the appropriateness of a sentence is in many respects determined by the way in which the sentence was chosen. Justification of an imposed sentence is an integral part of this process, as it expresses the application of principles within a specific case and context. For similar reasons, sentencing scholarship prefers a consistency of approach to a consistency of outcome (Harris, 2022, pp. 34–38), setting the priority on how the sentence was reached and not primarily on whether the "correct" sentence was imposed.

Providing detailed justification for an imposed sentence is essential for any sentencing system which strives to apply and develop sentencing principles or to take a so-called principled sentencing approach (von Hirsch et al., 2009). From the onset, principled sentencing scholarship has argued that in sentencing, an essential part is played by judges, who are required to give the reasons for the sentences they impose (Morris, 1977). But why? Principled sentencing requires that all factors be considered individually and then collectively. The process of reaching the decision should be reviewable and repeatable, leading to similar conclusions. Additionally, the sentence should be comparable to theoretical conclusions. Achieving these goals is either impossible or complicated without sentencing decisions being properly motivated; one cannot review the thought process, repeat it, generalise it or make sure that all factors were considered without the reasons being explicitly mentioned. However, surprisingly, the way in which judges should provide reasoning has not been thoroughly considered and systematically examined within the sentencing scholarship. This book tries to remedy this issue.

DOI: 10.4324/9781003470670-1

"Let's provide reasons for decisions taken by judges!" is certainly not a new idea; it has been repeated since the end of the 18th century. Prior to the Enlightenment period, the reasons for sentencing were not communicated so that the sovereign's authority would not be lessened (Cohen, 2015; Ferrand, 2011). Yet when rationality began to replace faith, and the important point was not *who* made the decision but whether the decision was *correct*, the role of motivation acquired greater significance. Additionally, as decisions began to be reviewed by higher courts, written provision of reasoning became a necessity (Bobek, 2010).

Whatever the discussion over the last two centuries has been concerning the necessity of providing reasoning and whatever the legal requirements of providing reasons for sentences set by different codes of criminal procedure, the current practice is not encouraging. In common-law countries, where reason-giving should be encouraged since it enables the formation of a common law of sentencing (Morris, 1977), the reasons are not provided even if the legislator mandates them to be. For example, in Massachusetts, federal district courts provided either no reasons at all or only very general reasoning (which amounts to no reasoning) in 57.7% of cases in which they were obliged to do so (Scott, 2013). A study examining reason-giving at two Dublin courts discovered that the courts gave reasons orally (no written opinions were required) in only 32% of cases as well as in only 42% of cases where a custodial sentence was imposed (Hamilton, 2005). In England and Wales, evidence from 12 magistrate courts suggests that in 60% of cases, the statement of reasons was not provided properly or not at all (Burney, 1985) and both the crown and magistrate courts only rarely showed a complex consideration of all factors (Ewart & Pennington, 1988).

The situation does not seem to be much better in continental legal systems, where judges are usually provided with broad discretion without being offered guidance via sentencing guidelines, guiding judgments or starting points (with a few exceptions, such as the Netherlands and Finland). In Germany, for example, it has been shown that "the reasons given in the opinion are largely unrelated to the sentence actually imposed," while Swiss judges evaded appeal by listing all the factors without specifying what weight they carry (Hassemer, 1983; Killias, 1994, p. 22). Similarly, in Kosovo, judges usually enumerate the factors without disclosing what role they play and how they arrived at the conclusion (OSCE, 2010).

Judges across the globe (or at least across the global North) have been ignoring the requirement to provide reasons for the sentences they impose for a long time. There are two possible explanations for this: a substantive explanation and a procedural explanation. First, judges might be generally reluctant to disclose their reasoning because they are unsure about why they made their decisions.[1] If this is so, then we need to develop sentencing theories in greater detail and communicate them better to judges so that they can have a better idea about why they made a decision. There might, however, be another – procedural – explanation: judges might not know how to present and structure their reasoning when they impose sentences. If judges are simply instructed "to provide reasons" but are not told how to do it, it is unreasonable to expect high-quality sentence justifications. If this second explanation is at least partially correct, we need to develop a theory of how sentence justification and its basic elements (can) operate and suggest how they should be translated into practice.

These substantive and procedural issues are likely interconnected; to struggle for principled sentencing means to aim for better-motivated sentences. It is impossible to develop one without it influencing the other. While the substantive sentencing scholarship has been greatly developed over the last decades, the discussion of the procedural aspects has been seriously neglected. The aim of this book is thus to develop in detail a theory of providing reasons for sentences, test this theory in different countries and suggest very specific ways of how it can be implemented in practice.

Following this Introduction, Chapter 2 sees Jakub Drápal make a strong case for providing detailed reasoning for imposed sentences from a criminological, legal and behavioural perspective. Understanding why a sentence was imposed is crucial not only for the two key figures of criminal proceedings – the offender and the victim – but also for the public, as it increases judicial legitimacy and public acceptance. Furthermore, a fair and just sentencing system cannot control and improve itself without reason-giving; appellate, supreme and constitutional courts cannot review the decision without reasoning of a high quality, and attempts should be made to analyse sentencing practice with the aim of evaluating it and forming a common law of sentencing. Finally, providing reasons for an imposed sentence is also beneficial for the quality of the decision and the judges; the necessity to express the reasons which justify a decision encourages the judge to deliberate about the case, the roles of individual principles and the subtle differences between individual cases.

There are of course also several arguments why judges should not provide reasons for the sentences they impose. Transparency incites discussion; the criticism of judicial decisions might thus be more frequent if judges express why they made a specific decision, possibly decreasing judicial legitimacy. Legal realists might suggest that reasoning will always be artificial as it is carried out after the sentence is imposed, not prior to it. Moreover, providing reasoning for all the sentences might be ineffective, barring judges from more important tasks. Chapter 2 – and to a lesser extent also the other chapters

1 A less optimistic explanation is that judges do not want others to know the real reasons for their decisions.

– argues, however, that these points are not sufficiently important to tilt the scales in favour of not providing reasons for imposed sentences. Their implications for sentence justifications and the realistic expectations we should have for them are discussed.

In Chapter 3, Pauline Schuyt and Jakub Drápal develop a theoretical framework relating to sentence justification. Specifically, they outline three basic principles sentence justifications need to fulfil in order to be understandable and reproducible. First, the factors influencing sentence imposition need to be explicitly identified and courts need to specify what shape they should take; it is, for example, not sufficient to mention that the defendant has previous convictions, but the extent of these convictions needs to be discussed in detail. Second, the importance of each factor needs to be expressed; in other words, does the factor play an aggravating or mitigating role and, if so, how strongly does it influence the sentence? Third, all factors need to be weighed against each other for a final decision to be reached. Only fulfilling all three principles will lead to sentence justifications of sufficiently high quality. Chapter 3 closes the book's first part, which focuses on the theoretical side of sentence justification.

In the second part of the book, we focus on evaluating reason-giving for first-level and appellate courts from the perspective of the three basic principles summarised above and explicated in Chapter 3. We do so by examining in detail the reasons given for sentences in Czechia, Estonia, Moldova, Slovakia and Slovenia. There are two reasons why we focus on this post-communist region. First, the role of sentence justification is crucial for systems in this region, as most of them have not yet held a thorough debate on structuring sentencing discretion. Second, the current conditions resemble in many ways the discretion judges were provided with at the beginning of the 19th century. As of current practice, there is a list of mitigating and aggravating factors, rules for imposing specific sanctions are defined in very general terms, there is not much assistance from the Supreme Court in interpreting the role of individual factors, and sentencing guidelines, guideline judgments, starting points or any other measures aimed at increasing the principled nature and unification of the imposed sentences are absent (Drápal & Plesničar, 2023).

As a result of these circumstances, post-communist judges are provided with a high level of discretion, the use of which cannot be understood without sentence justification. There are no other measures such as starting points or sentencing guidelines that might suggest why a judge took a specific decision. The reasoning provided for the chosen sentence is thus the only place where the judge is accountable for the use of the very broad discretion with which he or she is provided. Neither the defendant nor the public or the prosecutor may receive information about why the specific sanctions were imposed if judges do not provide detailed reasons for their decisions. Chapter 4 thus discusses in detail the quality of reasons given for sentences in these five post-communist countries, and shows how an important majority of decisions do not fulfil the three basic principles outlined in Chapter 3. Additionally, researchers from these countries have noted that typically, court decisions mention sentencing aims only superficially, as the simple reference to a sentencing aim often does not lead judges to discuss factors which reflect the mentioned sentencing aim.

First-level courts' decisions are reviewed by appellate courts, who are frequently mentioned within sentencing scholarship as an actor that can develop sentencing principles (the common law of sentencing) and significantly unify sentencing practice. In Chapter 5, Jakub Drápal and Tomáš Vanča firstly discuss why such expectations are unreasonable and then provide a detailed account of how Czech appellate courts decide on sentences. Within the theoretical part of the chapter, they present (i) the concepts of the standard of review – what level of error is necessary for an appellate court to interfere – and (ii) the method of review – how appellate courts review sentences. They conclude that if first-level courts provide reasoning of low quality and appellate courts primarily (only) correct excesses, it is improper to expect appellate courts to create a common law of sentencing.

This case study on Czech appellate courts discloses that, in a system with broad judicial discretion and unclear sentencing principles, it is unreasonable to expect appellate courts to develop any principled sentencing jurisprudence. Appellate courts thus interfere not only when excessive sentences are imposed by first-level courts – in line with the legislative provisions in Czechia – but also when they consider a sentence to be simply improper. In addition, they try to develop sentencing principles, yet – for the lack of theoretical sentencing scholarship – these theories are often oversimplified or erroneous. Chapter 5 concludes by outlining the conditions necessary for appellate courts to contribute to principled sentencing and by suggesting a standard of review for a sentencing system rooted in a proportionalist paradigm. Chapter 5 closes the second part of the book by examining the reasons provided by courts of different levels.[2]

In the third – final – part of the book, we debate the possible pathways towards increasing the quality of sentence justifications. We begin by mentioning experiences of a country that has repeatedly tried to improve the quality, although so far unsuccessfully: in Chapter 6, Sonja Meijer discusses the developments and measures taken in the Netherlands to improve the quality of sentence justifications. The Netherlands is one of a few countries – if not the only country – that has already developed, applied and tested several measures aimed at improving the quality of sentence justifications. These efforts, however, have not yet resulted in high-quality sentence justifications. The chapter discusses both the possible reasons for this failure and the current

2 The reasons provided by courts for parole decisions have also been examined in Czechia (Drápalová & Drápal, 2022), but as this book focuses on front-end sentencing and develops principles for front-end sentencing, these are not discussed.

discussions about how sentence justification could be further improved. The Dutch experience thus reminds readers thinking about possible improvements what means were tested – and why they failed.

The book is concluded by Jakub Drápal in Chapter 7, in which he discusses what sentence justification might look like in practice. Jakub argues that such sentence justification should guide judges to consider all necessary information; this enables them to fulfil the three principles outlined in Chapter 3 and to clarify why a specific decision was made. Taking inspiration from England and Wales and Sweden, the chapter discusses both general principles, which should shape sentence justification, and their possible application to a Czech context, as every application of sentence justification needs to be country-specific. The presentation of a sentencing protocol – a form which guides judges to make a principled and transparent decision – serves as an example of the practical application of the theoretical principles discussed in the first part of the book. Such an approach is consistent with the continental European sentencing tradition of employing less intrusive mechanisms in guiding courts' sentencing practices, if an improvement is sought. If the suggested sentencing protocol is applied in practice, judges will retain full discretion, yet they will be required to show how they used this tool.

Finally, it is important to note that this book broadly adheres to the principled sentencing paradigm, while acknowledging some of its deficiencies. Using the terminology of the legal theorist Aarnio, principled sentencing is a "form of life," meaning the standards and values which are shared within a community (Feteris, 2017). Thus, while some sentencing scholars view sentencing more as a craftwork (Tata, 2007), an art (Schachar, 1991) or a result of an instinctive synthesis (Hutton, 2006), we take a different approach. While we agree with some of their criticisms or conclusions – sharing some family resemblances in Aarnio's terminology – an agreement with these strands of sentencing scholarship would be hard to reach due to the different paradigms employed.

The key similarity in our approaches is that we aim to construct a more rational, accountable and transparent system of sentencing jurisprudence (Hutton, 2006) that satisfies the audience through reason-giving (Tata, 2007). The key difference lies primarily in the level of "real" reasons which judges are able to provide for their decisions. We argue that judges should be able to provide rather detailed reasons, disagreeing with an approach that reason-giving should not be "mainly a cognitive exercise in the application of normative penal philosophy" (Tata, 2020, p. 69). A second difference would probably consist in why we consider sentence justification important; for us, the most important factor is the identification of reasons justifying the sentence that might later be criticised, appealed or generalised, not the satisfaction of the audience. On a more crude level, we might say that reason-giving is important for us primarily from a legal perspective, not a sociological one. This is both a strength and a weakness of our approach.

2 Reasons for (and against) justifying sentences

Jakub Drápal

Introduction

Sentence justification is one of the cornerstones of modern sentencing systems. Rule of law requires judges to be accountable and their decisions to be reviewable. In sentencing scholarship, there has been a substantial movement in favour of defining "principled sentencing" – a set of principles according to which sentences should be imposed – and there is a consensus that such principled sentencing necessarily relies on sentence justification (Morris, 1977). Principled sentencing is unachievable without each case being expressly distinguished and without a discussion of how its particular features impact sentence imposition. Appellate courts, supreme courts and sentencing councils or committees cannot reasonably decide on individual cases or, for that matter, analyse jurisprudence and provide sentencers with guidance if judges fail to provide reasoning for the sentences they impose. More broadly, the legitimacy of the imposed sentences as viewed by offenders, victims and the public depends upon how well those sentences are explained. In justifying the decisions they make – in which they apply the law and not their personal opinion – judges are entrusted with wide powers. However, despite occupying such a seemingly unshakeable position, disclosing the reasoning behind any given sentence is by some still viewed as dangerous, impractical, impossible or overly burdening and time-consuming.

In this chapter, I summarise and develop rationales both for and against sentence justification from criminological, legal and behavioural perspectives. Since the criminal justice system focuses primarily on offenders and victims, I begin by discussing why sentence justification is crucial for these parties. With authorities' roles diminishing in today's era of pluralism, the rationalisation and legitimisation of decisions is becoming ever more important, as it enables the criminal justice system to preserve or re-acquire legitimacy and judges to retain wide discretion in sentencing. If sentences are not individually justified, to study sentencing practice and the principles underlying it is demanding. Thus, I further discuss behavioural research on dual-process thinking, which stresses the importance of detailed justification for

DOI: 10.4324/9781003470670-2

high-quality decision-making and suggests that judges should be nudged in specific ways when they justify sentences.

Both these noble and practical rationales play heavily in favour of sentence justification. Some, however, have argued that justification cannot attain these goals, and several other dissenting voices have suggested that judges should either provide reasons in a limited way or not at all. I discuss their reasons for this view and what they see to be the difficulties and undesirable consequences of justifying imposed sentences. I close the chapter with a realistic view of sentence justification, maintaining its importance while also responding to the identified obstacles.

Importance for the offender and victim

Criminal sanctions are the strongest possible official intrusions into our lives. Since freedom represents the highest value of which a modern state might deprive its citizens,[1] it is only reasonable to expect any powers to restrict it to be used in a transparent and accountable way. Thus, any measure that leads to a more transparent decision on criminal sanction is beneficial (Samuels, 1981). The bottom line here is that offenders simply deserve to know why their rights are taken away (Burgess, 2017; Cassidy & Ullmann, 2016).

The consequences of unjustified sentences clearly illustrate the importance of reasoning. Imagine being sentenced without justification. Was the sentence imposed in line with legal rules, and was it properly individualised? Should you appeal against, or be grateful for the sentence imposed? You have little on which to ground that decision: you are aware that some information was inputted, but you have no indication of whether this information was considered or how it was processed. The correctness of the sentence itself does not stem from the justification and elaborated argumentation, but from the authority of the judge; however, can you accept that authority if the judge has not bothered to give any explanation of why your freedom is to be restricted? Does the judge care about you as a human being?

Feelings like these can hamper the communication of censure to offenders, which is one of the most vital elements in the criminal justice system (du Bois-Pedain & Bottoms, 2019). Criminologists have long argued that offenders are willing to accept harsher sanctions when their reasoning is explained; on the contrary, when no justification is provided, offenders tend to resent them (Berkowitz, 1974; Samuels, 1981). Procedural justice research has emphasised this point in recent decades: an understanding of what is going on and trust in the person making the decision are both of paramount importance in determining whether the offender perceives the decision as fair, correct

1 Except in the few Western countries that still impose capital punishment.

and just (Tyler, 1988, 2003, 2007). No one likes to be criticised or deprived of their rights, yet it is much easier to resent an unjustified censuring decision than one that is explained in detail.

When we are not only told what to do, but are also told why, our human dignity is preserved: the provision of reasoning signals to us that we are important to the decision-maker who is treating us with respect (Schauer, 1995). In terms used by Martin Buber (Buber, 1970), providing detailed justification for an imposed sentence establishes an "I–You" relationship, a relationship between two persons, whereas simply imposing the sentence without any explanation of why that decision was taken establishes an "I–It" relationship, in which the offender is an object. The latter approach by definition complicates censure communication – or indeed communication at all.

Any relationship between two persons inherently implies at least a limited amount of care for one another. The censuring message of a sentence not only communicates disapproval but can also serve as a guiding principle for future crime-free behaviour (Samuels, 1981). Hence, an appropriate and justified sentence can offer the offender a way out of their criminal career; this is far harder to achieve if the sentence is unjustified. This logic is already present in our justice systems: a ruling by the Czech Constitutional court stipulates that, when dismissing parole, judges must indicate not only the reasons for rejecting parole, but also how the offender can improve his/her chances of obtaining parole in the future.[2] In other words, sentence justification is not solely about explaining what was done wrong and how it is to be punished, but also a means of providing guidance for the offender's future.

Thorough sentence justification further enables judges to communicate to offenders that although they should feel guilty for their (criminal) actions, they need not be ashamed of themselves as human beings. That is an important message both from a philosophical viewpoint – we are condemning the offender for what he or she committed, not for who he or she is – and from a pragmatic one: criminological research suggests that offenders who feel guilty re-offend less, while those who feel ashamed of themselves re-offend more (Hosser et al., 2008; Tangney et al., 2011, 2014). Proper justification induces the right feelings of guilt while limiting the counterproductive effects of shame. While justification should not be idealised or overemphasised, it is one of the few instruments available to the criminal justice system that can persuade offenders to accept their sentences and make changes to their behaviour in future.

While the offender is traditionally the centre of attention in modern criminal proceedings, victims have long played rather marginal roles in the process. Even today, victims are often provided with limited information about the

2 Decision of the Constitutional Court n. II. ÚS 482/18 on 28.11.2018, point 58; the author contributed to this decision as an assistant to the judge-rapporteur.

criminal proceedings and are seldom represented by attorneys. Their insight into how criminal law or sentencing operates is often rather poor. However, since they are in the position of having been harmed and having yielded their right to revenge for the harm they endured to society (via the criminal justice system), victims do need to understand the state's reaction to the offence they have suffered. Victims may easily have the impression that the response is insufficient if judges fail to explain the reasoning behind the sentences imposed, especially if they do not mention the harm caused to the victim. Sentence justification communicates, at the very least, the message that the judge has thoroughly considered the case. Victims may not agree with their decision but ought to at least feel that they have not been ignored.

Detailed justification is particularly important when the sentences imposed are highly likely to be viewed by victims as too lenient. One example of this is the imposition of suspended prison sentences without probation, which are the most common form of sanction in Central and Eastern Europe (Krajewski, 2007, 2016). This sanction has widely been portrayed as letting the offender walk free (Bartels, 2010; Freiberg, 2019). Judges are often criticised by victims and the media if they impose it in cases involving more serious crimes, such as rape: it is seen as both inadequate and disproportionate and often as evidence of judges not taking sexual violence seriously. Frequent criticism of this sort, which we have seen for example in the Czech Republic in recent years, is at least partially driven by a lack of thorough sentence justification from Czech judges (see Chapters 4 and 5). When the sentence is not properly justified, the victim and other audiences may not appreciate the judge's reasons for choosing a suspended prison sentence. The Czech Penal Code stipulates that after deciding that a prison sentence is to be imposed, the decision as to whether that sentence should be suspended or not should be based on whether the judge can expect the offender to lead a law-abiding life.[3] The severity of the offense and its impact on the victim is not a deciding factor for this aspect of the sentence. However, since this rule is rarely mentioned in judges' reasoning, it is also rarely mentioned by the critics of such sentences.

Would it help crime victims to know that suspended sentences – viewed by many as laughable – are imposed due to a possible structural deficiency, rather than because the harm done to them was not considered serious? It might, because it would tell them that if there is something amiss it is amiss on a general level and does not represent a misjudgement of the details of their case or the seriousness of the offence and harm they suffered. Better provision of sentence justification might thus prevent – or at least reduce – secondary victimisation, even if that justification cites system deficiencies. Since victims cannot usually appeal against the sentence, knowing that a suspended sentence was issued for systemic rather than case-specific reasons enables

3 Section 81(1) of the Czech Penal Code.

them to fight against the perceived leniency in a different way: by pushing for possible legislative change. In other words, justification enables people to take the problem up with the legislator, opening the door to possible improvements, rather than being angry at a specific judge, who may actually have had little choice.

Judicial legitimacy and public acceptance

Modern societies are built on the concept of rationality. Judges' detailed explanation of their reasoning is one of the best representations of such rationality. Judges are given unique authority and powers, for which they have to account. The public, based on that reasoning, places its trust in the judiciary and expects it to exercise the powers entrusted to it (Kremnitzer, 1991; Stewart, 2009), preventing speculation over cabinet justice. If explanations are not provided, "a new generation of 'beliefs', 'tools', 'techniques', 'bargains' and cynical explanations may be generated" (Miller, 1989, p. 21). Justice must not only be done; it must also be seen.

Justified decisions are necessary for the public to view judges as legitimate actors in the modern criminal justice system. Unlike the legislative branch, judges do not derive their legitimacy from elections, nor are they responsible to such elected representatives, as is the executive branch of the government. Given that the judiciary is not elected, judges – in the vast majority of countries – do not have political responsibility (Cohen, 2015). Judicial legitimacy thus cannot be founded on external authority, but rather on the persuasiveness of their decisions. The judiciary must earn the population's trust, which is not granted automatically (Schuyt, 2010, Chapter 3.1). Proper justification of their decisions is one of the best measures judges can take to ensure that they continue to be entrusted with extensive powers and regarded as authorities. This holds true especially for sentencing, since judges typically operate with a wide discretion regarding both the type and extent of the sanctions they might impose (Chanenson, 2006). The more discretion judges have, the more accountable they need to be.

If judges fail to exercise the discretion entrusted to them in a transparent and principled way, primarily by providing detailed sentence justifications, it is very easy for legislators to limit that discretion, for example through restrictive measures such as numerical sentencing guidelines, or indeed strip judges of it altogether (Schuyt, 2010, Chapter Epilogue). If judges do not justify their use of the most intrusive tools the state possesses, it could quite easily be argued that judges should not be wielding such powers. Proper justification is a key instrument to retaining discretion, as it enables the judiciary to demonstrate the importance of individualisation by presenting their reasoning in cases which at first sight might seem similar, but which require different sentences to be imposed.

Sentence justification can not only positively enhance trust in the judiciary; it can also reduce negative perception of sentencing discretion by limiting its misuse and providing fewer opportunities for critics to misinterpret judicial decisions as abusive of that discretion. Sentence justification further serves as a safeguard against misuse of power in individual cases, as some decisions simply cannot be justified and, when reasoning is provided, these can be easily rectified on an appeal. By specifying reasons for the decisions, judges are able to better answer to those who claim that judges have abused the powers entrusted to them.

In a homogeneous society in which everyone agrees on the underlying sentencing principles, a simple announcement of the imposed sanction might be sufficient. However, in a post-modern pluralistic society in which people hold different opinions on, for example, sentencing rationales, we might not necessarily agree with either the decision itself or the reasons given for it and are unlikely to even agree with one another (Cohen, 2015). Reason-giving becomes essential, since societal acceptance of any decision directly depends upon the quality of the discussion and of the justification. Modern legal theorists such as Jürgen Habermas, Robert Alexy or Aulius Aarnio have suggested that justification is not an option but a requirement for any legitimate decision (Feteris, 2017, pp. 91, 118, 155–156). The outcome is legitimised by the process (Bobek, 2010), and an inherent part of that process is the justification of the outcome.

The visibility of justice being done is of paramount importance in criminal matters, and this cannot be achieved without transparent decision-making (Stürner, 2011). This is true especially in sentencing. The public largely understands what theft or fraud is; when a continental judge simply recounts what happened and what evidence serves as proof, there is often little need for any more thorough justification connecting the evidence to the decision on guilt. However, to understand why a specific sentence has been imposed can sometimes be harder. An explanation of the judge's reasons for choosing a given sentence is thus essential if that sentence is to be understood, and thereby accepted by the public.

Proper functioning of the system

Judicial review by appellate, supreme and constitutional courts

The judicial system is designed pragmatically; everyone is aware that judges sometimes make mistakes and that they hold a variety of different opinions, which may lead them to various conclusions. Their mistakes need to be rectified, and their differing views require unification. Appellate courts address both of these matters by ruling on both factual and legal questions, while supreme courts interpret the law and constitutional courts serve as the last safeguard of human rights. The raison d'être of these higher courts is to review the decisions made by courts of lower instances.

When deciding on an appeal against a sentence, courts are usually responding to one or more arguments that a specific factor was wrongfully applied; that all of the factors were incorrectly weighted, resulting in an unjust sentence; or that the presented evidence was insufficient. If the sentence was not properly justified by the first-level court, it is not only impossible for the higher courts to review that decision, but it also actually makes it rather difficult to even file an appeal at all. Unless the court that imposed the sentence explains what factors were considered, what kind of evidence was used to establish them, what role the individual factors played and how they were weighted (Ho, 2000; Schuyt, 2010, Chapter 3.2.2; Slawsky, 1990; Stewart, 2009), the possibilities of (successfully) filing an appeal are greatly limited.

If a decision made by a lower court is not justified, the higher court tasked with reviewing that decision can – at best – decide anew and state the reasons for its decision. This approach to appeal robs the offender of a proper, principled review and denies the higher court any opportunity to review the lower court's decision or the principles upon which it was based. In such situations, higher courts are further likely to be reluctant to interfere with the sentences imposed by lower courts as they often review only the case file; this provides the lower courts with some leeway and means that only their most clearly visible transgressions are corrected.

Clarification of sentencing principles is thus unimaginable without thorough sentence justification. When the application of sentencing principles in a specific case is not clearly stated, it is impossible to identify (i) what sentencing principles were considered and (ii) how they were interpreted. Imagine that a lower court sentences an offender who was convicted 10 years ago for assault and imposes a sentence that is substantially more severe due to that previous conviction. If the lower court does not mention its consideration of the previous conviction or mentions only generally that it considered previous convictions among many other factors without specifying how, it becomes extremely difficult for a higher court to rule on whether that previous conviction should be taken into account and, if so, then how much it should influence the sentence.

Appellate, supreme and constitutional courts usually have the power to strike down decisions made by lower courts if they are not properly justified. The rationale behind this rule is clear: unless the lower courts enable a review of their decisions, higher courts will be unable to properly fulfil their duties. In theory, this means that higher courts could easily begin to require more detailed reasoning from lower courts in practice. Yet there are several reasons why higher courts are reluctant to do so. Higher-court judges tend to sympathise with lower-court judges, as most of them began their judicial practice at lower courts. They are well aware of how dreadfully hard to explain sentence selection might be, so they might feel it reasonable to demand a very detailed reasoning. Furthermore, if higher courts were to insist on lower courts explaining their decisions in greater detail, the higher courts would then have to justify their own decisions on appeals in equal detail, or at least be prepared to do so. Alternatively, if most lower-court decisions are poorly justified, it could be that higher-court judges feel helpless. Sudden quashing of the majority of decisions might – at least temporarily – overload the courts and prevent justice from being done sufficiently quickly. Hence, while poorly justified lower-court decisions hamper the review process and while higher courts theoretically can instruct lower courts to thoroughly justify their sentences, in practice, higher courts are often reluctant to use this power.

Analysing the practice: unifying opinions, sentencing commissions and researchers

Even after decades of research, there is still no consensus in sentencing scholarship about how particular factors influence, or indeed should influence, sentence imposition. Even the most important factors, such as multiple crimes or previous convictions, were only thoroughly discussed in the last decade (Frase & Roberts, 2019; Roberts & von Hirsch, 2010; Ryberg et al., 2018), and empirical evidence of their use in practice is limited, especially outside common-law systems. Yet knowledge of what judges are doing is essential for any institution wishing to provide guidance for sentencers or to correct sentencing practices. For example, identifying factors relevant to sentencing is necessary for determining their influence on sentence imposition. Furthermore, in order to discover any areas in which practice contradicts theory, one first needs to know why sentencers are making certain choices.

In practice, judges do not always act as they claim. The sentence justifications judges provide do not necessarily represent the genuine reasoning behind their decisions. To some extent, this is unimportant. The system can play the judges' game: "You say you have considered this factor? OK, we'll give you guidance about how important that factor should be in similar situations." Once the system has provided guidance for all the factors that judges say they take into account and judges have complied with that advice, some unaccounted influences on the sentence might appear, signalling that judges either took some additional as-yet-unannounced factors into account or considered some existing factors improperly. Of course, this imagined procedure is overly idealistic; nevertheless, the sentencing principles mentioned by judges themselves constitute the best starting point for providing sentencing guidance. Once these principles have been thoroughly debated and their application in different situations specified, the system can begin to identify any factors judges (un)intentionally leave out of their justifications.

Analysis of the sentencing factors judges claim to consider can be carried out easily if their sentences are well justified. If they are not, the elaborated research required for such an analysis would be both costly and demanding. This applies both in common-law systems, where sentencing commissions usually study sentencing, and in the post-communist continental systems in which supreme courts can issue the so-called "unifying opinions." These opinions stipulate how a legal question – one that has been resolved differently by various lower courts – should be interpreted (in theory, not in relation to any actual case). If judges fail to provide reasoning for the sentences they impose, the supreme court is disabled from issuing unifying opinions on sentencing principles, as identifying variation in the application of individual principles is impossible. This example illustrates that even somewhat artificial justification can lead to system improvement. When the provided justification is only general or none at all, traditional legal measures to oversee principled sentencing have no alternative but to fail.

Where sentences are poorly justified, researchers are also limited in assessing current practices. If detailed reasoning is absent, it is much harder to, for example, code the factors that judges perceive as important in their decision-making to reveal the full variety of individual sentencing principles, or to analyse particular institutes, such as the custodial threshold. Faced with a lack of justification, researchers resort to simply asking judges about their views of different factors or to deducing why they might have made certain decisions via quantitative analysis of sentencing data. These methods are more demanding and have substantial limitations, hampering the researchers' abilities to explore judicial responses – or deliberation – under various circumstances. If sentencing decisions were properly explained, such research would be much easier, albeit not without limitations.

Judicial ethics and honesty

In certain jurisdictions, judges have a statutory duty to explain their decisions. Their explanations may be truthful or may present an artificial justification. According to U.S. Judge Kozinski (Kozinski, 1993), judges who are true to themselves and to their professions will try to make the reasons for their decisions as transparent as possible, since it is their ethical duty to do so. If they failed to do so, they would be viewed by other judges or by their own assistants as unfit for their job. Kozinski points out that if the judicial professions consider transparent reasoning the norm and its evasion as problematic, judges are placed under informal pressure to provide detailed justification for their decisions (Schauer, 1995). However, if judges consider it acceptable – or even worthy of pragmatic praise – to provide vague or no sentence justification (Killias, 1994) and thus to evade any possible control by an appellate court, it becomes much harder to enforce the requirement of proper sentence justification.

Further use of sentence justification

The court decision is often the only document other criminal justice agencies use. Prisons and probation services often have access to the judgment, but do not traditionally have an easy access to case files. If the decision is poorly justified, this means that these other criminal justice agencies are left without sufficient knowledge of why a certain decision was taken. Knowledge of this sort might, however, be of help during the execution of the sentence (Samuels, 1981). In the absence of reasoning, both courts and other criminal justice agencies thus either have to infer why the court made a particular decision or are deprived of the possibility to make their own decisions based on the court's opinions.

Possible examples of this type of situation are numerous. Prison services can use the information when making initial decisions about assigning offenders to groups within the prison. The justification might also influence probation or prison services in deciding which programs the offender should undergo. When deciding on parole, a well-justified decision would be of use to those deciding whether parole is deserved. In some systems, court decisions are used for additional purposes; for example, employers might be allowed to consider whether an applicant has a previous conviction, but to know whether to reject an applicant based on that conviction, they need to assess the seriousness of the offence and whether the sentence was sufficient. Without justification by the court, it becomes harder for other professionals than judges to do so. Finally, judges might need the reasoning when sentencing a repeat offender who has been previously sentenced only for some of the committed offences, since in such a situation the judge must decide whether the already imposed sentence was sufficient or whether an additional punishment should be imposed. Doing so without clearly stated reasons for the previous decision is highly demanding.

Nudges and other behavioural rationales for requiring detailed sentence justification

Making the judge think about the case

Judges have to process cases quickly. Guilty pleas, plea bargains and penal orders are some of the measures that enable judges to do so. Sentence justification is – by practitioners – usually not considered to be an essential part of the decision-making process, and cutting it short enables them to save precious time. Judges repeatedly mention that providing their reasons in writing is an inefficient use of their time. Behavioural research, however, suggests otherwise. If a judge cannot write a short justification for the sentence they have imposed, within a matter of minutes, then that decision was likely not sufficiently principled and presumably required more thorough consideration. This is because when a judge imposes a sentence, he or she needs to have already thoroughly considered all relevant factors, whether there is enough evidence for them, how they should be weighted and how the interaction of various factors influences the type of sanction to be imposed and its length.

This is the crux of principled sentencing. Once all these steps have been taken, all that remains is for the judge to write it down. That should not take long, since the reasoning has already been formulated in the judge's head, and it has an additional benefit: upon expressly stating his/her reasons on paper, the judge might realise that what sounded right in his/her head "won't write" (Cohen, 2015; Liu, 2018; Waits, 1983). Writing down detailed sentence justification is thus both proof that the sentence decision was properly contemplated and a means of verifying the judge's own train of thought.

It follows that it is highly advisable for any judge to note down on paper at least a basic outline of their justification prior to announcing any decision, using this task as an opportunity to check that all relevant factors have been considered and appropriately weighted (Cohen, 2015). Otherwise, the judge runs the risk of finding out, when attempting to justify a decision that was already announced, that a different decision should in fact have been taken. A requirement to provide proper sentence justification should logically lead to more detailed consideration of the case and, consequently, to more appropriate sanctions (Burgess, 2017; Cohen, 2015; Ho, 2000; Stewart, 2009). It is hardly too much to demand from judges that they think all factors through thoroughly before making a decision that dramatically impacts the lives of those involved, comprising the most intrusive limitations that can be imposed on anyone's life.

The criminal justice system should therefore at the very least nudge judges to prepare reasoning for any sentences they impose before they officially impose them. Judges might, for example, be provided with a checklist of factors they should consider prior to taking any sentencing decision and nudged to briefly note down how each individual factor should be considered and weighted. Such a checklist might be based on reasoning requirements provided by a code of criminal procedure or it might summarise factors of relevance as mentioned in the criminal code. I provide an example of what this checklist might look like in Chapter 7. A formalised requirement of this sort would likely improve the quality of judicial reasoning, since psychological studies show that people believe the reasoning they give is more detailed than it actually is (Lombrozo, 2012). A checklist or similar initiative could thus be beneficial both for early-career judges, who might not be aware of all the factors they need to consider, and for more experienced judges, who might tend to overlook certain factors when their sentencing becomes too automated.

With such a tool in use, to suppose that justification would reach at least a certain minimum quality threshold is reasonable. This would be especially useful in continental legal systems, in which judges decide on guilt and on sentencing at the same time. Guilt is of paramount importance, and parties focus primarily on (dis)proving it. Given the "goal looms larger" effect, according to which people tend to act more rashly when the end comes closer (Molden & Higgins, 2012), when a continental judge is satisfied with the evidence regarding guilt, he or she might tend to close the case as quickly as possible. Nudges, such as the checklist proposed, can remind judges not to finish up too quickly at the expense of a high-quality, principled sentencing decision.

Recognising patterns

How do we determine that one sentence is needed rather than another? We first have to identify the factors distinguishing the case and then determine whether these factors justify imposing a particular sentence. Unless sufficient time and attention is paid to recognising these differences and deliberating their importance, proper differentiation of cases becomes difficult or impossible.

Psychological scholarship investigating the deliberation process identifies two types of thinking, which operate at different speeds: a more intuitive type 1 and a more reflective type 2. The latter consists in considering counterexamples, which is slower and more demanding and requires the use of working memory (Evans, 2012). Type 2 deliberation is needed for principled sentencing, for which being able to distinguish between sub-variations of cases is essential. Explanations are usually expressed as contrasts: we justify our ideas based on comparison with counterfactuals (Lombrozo, 2012), since it is by specifying and explaining the differences between groups that we define general underlying principles (Lombrozo, 2012; Schauer, 1995). Interestingly, those who explain more are more likely to identify subtle regularities underlying the category structure (Lombrozo, 2012). Yet it is unclear whether justifying sentences leads to a better distinction between principles, as to improve in an activity requires feedback, evaluation, training and opportunities for repetition and gradual refinement (Feltovich et al., 2018). Further, learning takes place via explicit differentiation followed by corrective feedback (Ericsson, 2018; Mosier et al., 2018), possibly provided by appellate courts (the quality of whose decisions is, however, often low; see Chapter 5).

In other words, the very process of justifying sentences likely enables judges to recognise patterns and differences between cases and offenders. Explicitly explaining the differences between cases should help judges to identify different categories and apply certain principles in their sentencing. In a functional criminal justice system, this would be built into judges' continuing training and practice: judges would be trained initially in how to justify sentences and their everyday practice would ensure repetitive realisation of this skill. Appellate courts would provide feedback when patterns were not properly recognised. Altogether, this would lead to more principled sentencing across the system.

Being consistent and reducing bias

Once a judge decides on a sentence and announces it in writing, he or she commits to deciding further cases in a similar manner (Schauer, 1995). A desire for internal coherency in our decision-making may be one of the main reasons why we justify our decisions at all (Chater & Oaksford, 2012). The alternative of treating similar cases differently would be the very definition of injustice and irrationality, and we inherently want to behave rationally and justly – or be seen to. If a judge openly states that a particular factor influenced his or her sentence choice in a specific way, they are likely to do so in future cases too, which reduces sentencing disparities.

A multitude of studies have shown that judges are influenced by extra-legal factors when sentencing, such as whether they are thinking about death (Arndt et al., 2005), whether they have similar names as defendants (Chen, 2017), or the shape of the offender's lips or nose in the case of African-Americans (King & Johnson, 2016).[4] Psychological literature has identified a wide palette of decision biases (LeBoeuf & Shafir, 2012). The idea behind sentence justification is that it should help eliminate such biases. Limited evidence suggests this holds true in practice: Liu (Liu, 2018) experimentally verified that if Chinese judges prepare their justification prior to making their decisions, the influence of bias decreases, although it does not disappear altogether. This result is to be expected and is in line with psychological literature suggesting that strong instructions can limit bias but not eliminate it altogether (Evans, 2012).

Non-directional thinking: a paradigm shift?

When deliberating over an issue, we are either motivated to reach a particular outcome (directional outcome) or we try to reach the most accurate outcome possible without knowing what that might be in advance (non-directional outcome, (Molden & Higgins, 2012). How do judges sentence? Do they first come up with a sentence they believe is appropriate instinctively and then look for reasons that justify that sentence, or do they consider all relevant factors in search of the most appropriate sentence?

In the first of these two possible decision-making procedures, judges would be less likely to consider any factors inconsistent with their desired sentencing outcome and would instead focus on factors that support it (Molden & Higgins, 2012). In other words, if a judge feels intuitively that the offender should be imprisoned, he or she will likely find reasons for imposing a prison sentence. The second, non-directional decision-making process is more suitable to achieve principled sentencing, since it implies consideration of all possible factors equally, with an open outcome. It is, however, not free of challenges, especially when pressure to conclude quickly is present: the motivation to come to a decision can lead to the judge considering an

4 For further examples, see e.g. (Goodman-Delahunty & Sporer, 2010).

insufficient amount of information and fixating on a particular factor, performing an over-simplified analysis and relying on stereotypical information (Molden & Higgins, 2012).

Judges should be trained not to look for reasoning that would support a sentence with which they have come up instinctively, but rather to search for an appropriate sentence based on their consideration of various factors. When doing so, they should not be pressured to make their decision quickly, since this could lead them to simplify their considerations. We do not know to what extent this entails a paradigm shift; there has been little research to date to show how judges come to their decisions (Spellman & Schauer, 2012).

Reasons for not providing reasons

There are a multitude of reasons why judges might not justify their decision. If one or more of these cannot be overcome, sentence justification might be seen as a futile exercise and an inefficient use of limited resources. We discuss the obstacles to justification one by one and debate whether judicial processes can be adjusted so that the benefits of justification prevail.

Nobody agrees with the reasons

Judges are often advised not to provide detailed reasons for their decisions. This is part of a tactic Judge Gertner has called "duck, avoid, and evade" (Gertner, 2016, p. 427). Lord Mansfield is famously known to have said: "Never give your reasons; – for your judgement will probably be right, but your reasons will certainly be wrong" (Campbell, 1873, p. 473; Ho, 2000). The only good thing about this being frequently cited is that it is equally frequently criticised as a relic of monarchist views which were common primarily between the eras of Enlightenment and rationalisation: in the 12th and 13th centuries, there was a belief that reasoning might display the weaknesses of a decision and open it up to refutation (Cohen, 2015).

Justifying ones' decisions is inherently risky, since that justification might be easily scrutinised, discussed or indeed disputed (Schuyt, 2010, Chapter Epilogue). The more details a judge provides, the more the offender, the prosecution, the public and the higher courts can criticise the individual steps leading to that decision (Schuyt, 2010, Chapter 3.3.2.2). This is best summarised by Scott and Schuyt:

> Writing a long opinion is asking for a trouble. A simple announcement from the bench or a terse written order gives the parties little to go on, and therefore little to attack.
>
> (Scott, 2013, p. 365)

A judge, who motivates little, has nothing to fear.

(Schuyt, 2010, Chapter 3.3.2.2)

However understandable this point of view might be, if taken seriously, it undermines the very essence of judging. If the primary judicial instinct is to evade judgment (which by definition includes making decisions based on reasons), this suggests a deeper problem with the judiciary's vision of its own role and with the education and training provided to judges. Moreover, given that judges usually hold tenured positions which entail high independence, prestige and income, the least society can expect of them is that they make their decisions transparent. As Kischel (2011) puts it, "[t]he fear of one's decision being subject to review is not a reason to lie" (p. 408).

Legal realists: post-hoc ergo artificial?

Why should we believe that the reasons a judge presents are the real reasons that led him or her to the decision? As legal realists have pointed out many times, the sentence justification the judge presents is only a posterior reconstruction of why a sentence was imposed, composed with the aim of strengthening the persuasiveness of the decision (Cohen, 2015; Hutton, 2006). Such claims are corroborated by psychological research expecting such a phenomenon to occur within the legal sphere (Spellman & Schauer, 2012).

While this criticism presents the most important substantive objection to the requirement of justifying sentences, reason-giving remains essential, even though we acknowledge its limitations. Everyone internally justifies the decisions they make, yet when we present those reasons externally, the justification might become distorted. Legal theorists Robert Alexy and Aulius Aarnio (Feteris, 2017, pp. 128, 161) focus on the playoff between internal justification (the real reasons leading to the decision) and external justification (the reasons presented), arguing that the aim of the legal system must be to achieve maximal accord between these two.

Systems might thus try to employ mechanisms that increase that accord, such as suggesting – or requiring – that judges write down an outline of their reasoning prior to imposing a sentence or that they write down their reasoning as soon as possible. Otherwise, it is much harder to rebut the argument that the justifications judges provide are retrospective reconstructions to create a "plausible account" (Hutton, 2006) rather than the genuine reasoning behind the sentence. An even more ambitious procedure would be to prepare a provisional written sentencing opinion one day before the sentencing hearing; the outcome might change depending upon an evidence presented at the hearing (Sweet et al., 1996). This idea, however, seems too demanding, given that many systems cannot make judges provide reasons for decisions they are currently making.

Pragmatic lawyers would be primarily concerned with whether the external justification is clear and detailed and whether it holds throughout the criminal procedure (Kischel, 2011; Schuyt, 2010, Chapter 3.4). As we cannot discover the inner process within a judge's mind, possible dissonance between the inner process and the external justification should not be at the centre of our attention. If the decision is properly justified and withstands all possible critique, then we need not worry about possible hidden reasons, since it is as close to an optimal sentencing outcome as possible. This is a fair view up to a point, but there is one problem: it is surely not sufficient for the decision to "survive" all possible appeals. That could be achieved, for example, by judges providing a whole multitude of reasons for a given decision, but without specifying their importance, as German and Swiss judges do (Killias, 1994). The decision has to be properly justified and reviewable and then be subjected to a critique.

Finally, even if we acknowledge that judges might at times provide fabricated post-hoc justifications for the sentences they have imposed, most judges believe that they do make their decisions in accordance with the principles set out by the legislator and jurisprudence. It might be beneficial to maintain this illusion (Berkowitz, 1974); when judges are trying to be subordinated to a legislator, they might be less subjective than if they were to decide openly according to their own beliefs. Similarly, it is important for the public to believe that judges are deciding – or at least trying to – within legal bounds and according to principles set out by the legislator.

Legal realists' critique thus suggests that a sentence justification serves a valid role so long as the discord between external and internal justification is not immense and the decision is reviewable. Various procedural measures can be employed to ensure that.

Typical whole case stories and different audiences

Cyrus Tata is the main contemporary critique of the legal-rational theory of justification. He first suggests that judges construct and present "typical whole case stories" instead of providing theoretical philosophical justifications that "suppose an asocial fixed reality of story" (Tata, 2002, p. 421, 2020, p. 69). This criticism does not necessarily contradict the legal-rational theory of justification, as legal scholars seeking to improve sentence justifications also argue that they should be presented as stories (Schuyt, 2010). The way forward might thus consist in presenting each case as a story to which sentencing principles are applied [see (Schuyt, 2010)]. The lack of a discussion of principles would be viewed suspiciously as Ho (2000) summarises it: "[O]ur tolerance for the 'impressionistic' type of reasoning is constrained by our fear of arbitrariness and irrationality and is limited by our desire for open justice" (p. 59).

Cyrus Tata does, however, also raise another obstacle to proper justification: according to him, judicial reasoning is often considered incoherent because it addresses very different audiences that require sentence justification to fulfil different roles (Tata, 2002, 2007, 2020, pp. 67–70). The reasoning needs to be understandable to the offender, who is often of lower-than-average intelligence; to the public, who require understandable yet legally distinguished formulations; and to an appellate court, which demands properly elaborated and often formal argumentation. The judge needs to respond to the offender's denial and the victim's and the public's emotions while maintaining professional distance and appearing impartial. Faced with these demands, a judge might simply decide against providing detailed reasoning as such.

While it is clearly true that judges communicate with diverse audiences in distinct ways, the solution is not to resign on sentence justification. Rather, different justifications might be given to different audiences. In continental legal systems, judges are usually obliged to provide their reasoning both orally and in writing. While the orally explained reasons might primarily appeal to the offender, the victim or the public by emphasising certain aspects and using particular wording, the written justification could primarily represent the legal-rational tradition. To provide only a few examples of how this might work, an acknowledgement of the harm caused to the victims, while essential, can be noted outside any justification of the imposed sentence. A simpler explanation might be communicated orally to allow the offender to understand the reasons behind it. In a widely followed case, a judge might publish a press report presenting the case and the decision in a way more understandable and accessible to the general public and press (Schuyt, 2010, Chapter 3.2.4). This would not be anything new; supreme and constitutional courts already publish summaries of their decisions on a daily basis.

Principled sentencing justification is imaginable even after we acknowledge the difficulties mentioned in this section. The judge needs to incorporate storytelling aspects in the justification process and address different audiences in diverse ways. I largely share Tata's view that reasoning primarily needs to be defensible (Tata, 1997, 2007). Nevertheless, in my conception, any written justification should be reserved for principled sentencing deliberation; it should include the true reasons – the reasons judge believes led him or her to the decision – expressed in a formal way. This written justification should explain why the decision was made in terms accessible to an audience with at least basic knowledge of the law. Unless the written sentence justification is principled in this way, the imposed sentence cannot be defensible.

Time demanding!

It is no surprise that doing anything properly takes time. The judiciary has limited time and is under constant pressure to close cases as quickly as possible. Spending additional time preparing a written decision with a detailed justification delays the closure of the case. Is it worthwhile spending that much time on reasoning (Cohen, 2015; Miller, 1989; Samuels, 1981)?

Scholars who have considered sentence justification previously largely agree that writing out the judges' reasoning should not take very long (Chanenson, 2006; Weinberg, 2014). One page, or at most two, of concise reasoning is sufficient for the judge to consider all relevant factors individually and explain their weight. If a judge has already thought about the individual factors and weighted them in their head, they should be able to write that thought process down easily. If they have not properly deliberated over what sentence should be imposed, the problem is not of insufficient time for issuing a written, principled sentence justification but of insufficient (time for) consideration of the relevant facts and sentencing principles.

Suppose it takes judges about half an hour to write down their reasoning on one to two pages. In the Czech Republic, where there were 75,141 criminal cases decided by 684 district and regional criminal judges in 2019 (Ministry of Justice, 2020),[5] this would have amounted to 37,570 hours (or 4,696 8-hour working days) spent on written sentence justification, in total. If we assume that the average judge works 230 days a year, written reasoning would take up 20.4 judge years, or approximately 3% of judges' total working time. This practice would not overburden Czech judges but is demanding enough on their time for the state to consider whether written justification should be provided in all cases, or whether simplified reasoning is acceptable in some cases.

The extent to which written justification might be simplified depends upon how well the criminal justice system functions at other points of the criminal proceedings. If the judge has thoroughly explained their decision orally, a hearing transcript might be viewed as a sufficient substitute for the written justification. This would, however, require the reasons given orally at the hearing to be detailed, well-structured and emotionless, which is not usually the case today (Miller, 1989; Scott, 2013). Moreover, it is unclear whether substituting the written justification with a transcript is in fact desirable, or whether the oral reasoning should address a different audience than the written one. Finding a middle road is thus not an easy task.

Shouldn't judges be viewed as authorities?

Requiring detailed sentence justification from judges would undeniably lead to public disappointment as the reasoning would often be problematic. Inevitably, some judges are suffering from burn-out, some are lacking sufficient intellectual capacities and some display pathological behaviours. Even the best judges sometimes make mistakes. One Czech judge who teaches sentencing to younger judges recently recounted one of his own mistakes. He had misheard the prosecutor's sentence recommendation and thought she was

5 Some regional judges serve at appellate courts, so the actual number of first-instance judges is lower.

suggesting a 300,000 CZK fine (approximately 12,000 €), while she was actually suggesting 30,000 CZK (1,200 €). To satisfy the prosecutor, he imposed a 100,000 CZK fine, even though otherwise he would have imposed a 30,000 CZK fine. The offender was horrified, the prosecutor surprised. Having realised his mistake, the judge admitted it, and the sentence was corrected by an appellate court.

Should these mistakes be visible? Some would think less of the judiciary since its authority would not be shrouded in mystery any more – judges would be brought down to the same level as other human beings, and their reasoning and deliberation would be easily criticised. Others would think more of judges for it; it is not easy to display one's weaknesses and open oneself to possible criticism. It is not easy to know whether to view judges as authorities is desirable (Hutton, 2015; Kremnitzer, 1991; Rawls, 1971). Most people would, if they ended up on trial, prefer to be sentenced by a judge whose mistakes (if any) are visible – and thus repairable – than by a judge whose authority is absolute and without review. We would also expect the judge's sentence justification to be meticulous: when someone's life is in the balance, we want to believe that the decision has been well considered.

In their justifications, judges should thus not resort to declaring they had no other choice but to impose a specific sentence (Gertner, 2016). Instead, they should emphasise that the decision was not taken lightly or intuitively and that all other options were carefully and systematically ruled out. Even advocates of the "instinctive synthesis" approach to sentencing unequivocally accept that it is necessary to provide reasons for sentencing (Hewton, 2010),[6] and those who claim that sentencing is primarily a "collective social and cultural practice" also require judges to show how their decisions are reached and persuade the audience of correctness of their decisions (Hutton, 2014, p. 4728). Judges who do not wish their authority to be challenged by "outsiders" (Hutton, 2006) might be best advised to reconsider their career choices.

A lack of flexibility or a lack of guidance?

The difficulty of justifying sentences in complex cases is that it might limit the sentencing options available to judges since the public might not understand the subtle differences between cases (Schauer, 1995). However, the very essence of written sentence justification is that it provides the factual basis for distinguishing the case in hand from other cases and presents the evidence for treating that case differently. While some members of the public might

6 To extent to which the decisions that are results of "instinctive synthesis" are really properly reasoned is a matter for further discussion and research since others have claimed that "instinctive synthesis … is not to further rational explanation. There is thus an element of the sacred" (Hutton, 2014, p. 4726).

not be persuaded by it, a detailed justification demonstrates that the judge has tried to individualise the sentence. As such, it in fact ensures that first-level judges retain substantial flexibility at sentencing. Detailed sentence justification limits the appellate court's ability to simply impose a sentence de novo. Instead, it forces the appellate court to respond to the original reasoning when making changes, thereby complicating the process of overturning the original sentence. If an appellate court overturns a well-justified sentence without appropriate argumentation, it is subject to professional ridicule. If a judge departs from the usual sentencing range, providing detailed reasons showing that the departure was warranted and needed, it is more persuasive than a general complaint that the legislator's sentencing ranges are limiting.

The last reason why proper sentence justification is a challenge is – in my view – the most important. It is the lack of sufficient sentencing guidance provided to first-level judges in particular – guidance as to how individual sentencing principles should be applied in practice. This complicates the preparation of any proper sentence justification as well as imposition of principled sentences. It is not sufficient for the legislator or higher courts to mention, for example, that previous convictions need to be considered; basic principles and the most important considerations for each factor need to be elaborated (Frase & Roberts, 2019). If the substantive penal law is not sufficiently developed, procedural aspects – including sentence justification – cannot fully compensate for it (Schoep, 2008).

If the expected influence of the most common factors on sentence choice is not generally defined, it is, nevertheless, possible for judges to arrive at a principled decision, albeit much harder for them to do so. Due to constant pressure to decide as fast as possible, many judges lack sufficient time and resources to deliberate over the various factors that influence sentencing. This results in a less principled and more intuitive decision, making it difficult to provide a principled justification ex post. It is not surprising that in such situations, appellate, supreme and constitutional courts would be reluctant to push first-level courts into providing detailed reasons for their sentence choices. This is a vicious circle that can only be broken through coordinated action and, in particular, the provision of better guidance for sentencers.

Realistic expectations of sentence justification

As I have discussed in this chapter, there are several concerns in relation to the practices involved in sentence justification that may result in judges providing reasoning that is less thorough, of lower quality or completely absent for the sentences they impose. These concerns can, however, be addressed to ensure that proper, full and principled justification is not only possible but is realisable in practice. If there is a tendency for justifications to give "ingenuine" reasoning, this might be acceptable as long as it is sufficiently detailed and the judge's discretion is accounted for. If justifications are being written ex post, after an intuitive decision, we could require judges to prepare their reasoning in advance and to use a checklist. If judges have a tendency to "tell stories" rather than focus on principles, sentence guidance can be adapted to address this. If there are several audiences to address, this need can be met by a range of diverse kinds of justifications: oral, written and press-briefing versions could be provided. If sentence justification is time-consuming, the scope of the justification could be reduced. If the state fails to provide sufficient guidance on sentencing to first-instance judges, that guidance can be formulated by the legislator, higher courts or academia. What this means is that we can be realistic about sentence justification while still expecting a requirement for detailed, principled reasoning to be upheld.

In all these various criticisms of the practicality of principled sentencing justification, we have not identified any issue that reasonably prevents judges from providing such justification. There are clearly some practical obstacles to be overcome, but since the need for detailed, principled sentence justification is supported by overwhelming evidence, the criminal justice systems must find the practical solutions that will enable sentences to be properly justified. In the following chapters, I and several knowledgeable colleagues analyse the decision-making of both first-level and appellate courts and suggest ways in which these various obstacles might be overcome.

3 Three stages of reason-giving

Identification, evaluation and weighing

Pauline Schuyt and Jakub Drápal

Introduction

The unstructured process of sentence imposition is highly complex. Judges are supposed to consider a multitude of numerous factors, consider various (possibly contradicting) sentence rationales and choose a specific combination of sanction types and their lengths from a myriad of possible combinations. For example, in Czechia, the criminal code and code of criminal procedure first require judges to consider approximately 70 factors in making their decisions; note that these factors might acquire various forms. Judges are required to impose a proportionate sentence (or a combination of sentences) while fulfilling rehabilitative, incapacitative and restorative aims. In most cases, Czech judges may choose between five types of main punishments – a fine, community work, home detention, suspended prison sentence and non-suspended prison sentence – which might be imposed alone, alongside each other or with other punishments such as various bans or obligations. We illustrate the complexity of this process in Figure 3.1.

Simply requiring judges to provide reasoning for their decisions – without providing them with any guidance on how to do it – will likely result in subpar reasoning. Similarly, requiring judges to decide without guidance will likely result in unprincipled and disparate decisions. This chapter presents three stages of reasoning necessary for judges to make a principled decision and for everyone else to understand why the court made a particular decision. Specifically, sentence reasoning should include three stages: (i) presenting what factors the court considers, requiring the judge to identify and specify what forms different factors acquire; (ii) deciding on their roles, namely whether they aggravate or mitigate the sentence decision and to what extent; and (iii) weighing all factors together to arrive at a final sentence. Within this chapter, we first discuss why such an approach is necessary, before providing a detailed presentation of each stage and concluding with a summary of the benefits of such reasoning.[1]

1 This chapter is based on Pauline Schuyt's PhD thesis (Schuyt, 2010, Chapters 11–12).

DOI: 10.4324/9781003470670-3

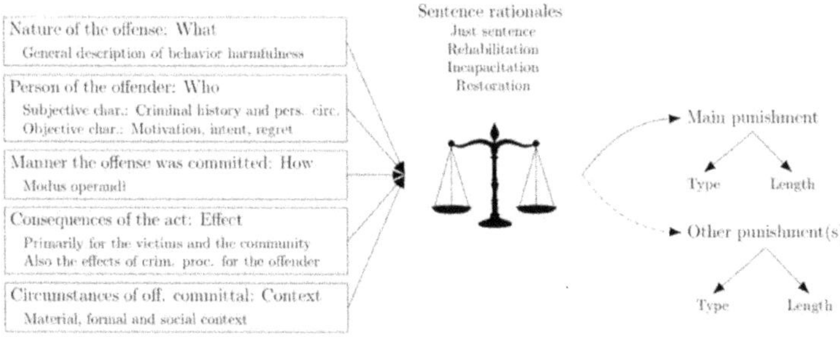

Figure 3.1 Complex process of imposing sentences

A myriad of factors and the deficits in considering them

Judges must consider a myriad of factors when sentencing an offender. We might illustrate their distinctiveness by dividing these factors into five categories according to a typical approach to storytelling: what was done, by whom, how exactly, with what effect and in what context. These categories define every story we experience as human beings. Judges seem no different as they construct offences and offenders as "whole case stories" (Tata, 1997, 2020, pp. 64–65). Dividing factors into such groups could be beneficial for considering different factors properly. An informal division also reveals the complexity of considering various aspects of the offence, the offender, the consequences of the act and the context in which it was committed.

First, judges ask *what* was committed, that is, the *nature* of the offence. The answer to this question does not directly relate to the consequences of the offence or the manner in which it was committed, but only sets the scene; it explains why behaviours of such type are harmful to society and in what ways. This exposé provides a starting point for the following discussion concerning what sentence should be imposed by broadly delineating the boundaries of what sentences might be appropriate for such behaviours.

Then, the leading actor enters the stage: *who* committed the offence? The person's behaviour is defined both by their objective and subjective characteristics. Objective characteristics relate to what can be ascertained from the outside, such as the criminal history or personal circumstances of the offender (such as family status or income). Subjective characteristics relate to the intent and motivation of the offender and, as such, can only be deduced from the outside. Subjective characteristics do not have to be limited to what happened before the committal of the offence. Still, they can relate, for example, to how the offender communicated their regret after the offence.

The modus operandi – *how* the offence was committed – provides an additional specification of the criminal behaviour. Offences (as classified within the relevant part of the penal code) are committed in various ways that increase or decrease their seriousness. For example, the use of a knife, committing the offence in a group and hurtful behaviour after having committed the crime all provide additional specifications of bodily harm. By describing how an offender committed an offence, judges show how a concrete case differs from similar cases, which enables them to impose a sentence individualised to the offence.

The main reason states criminalise a behaviour is on account of its harmfulness; judges thus need to pay special attention to the *effect* of the offence. Specifically, the consequences for the victims, their relatives and the community need to be evaluated. Display of these consequences acknowledges their pain; without it, they might feel abandoned, and the legitimacy of the criminal justice system acting on their behalf might be undermined. In explaining how these consequences influence sentence imposition, judges need to emphasise the link between the consequence and the intent; some consequences of the act might not have been intended by an offender and should, therefore, carry a different strength compared to the same consequences if intended. Additionally, the effect of the criminal proceedings on the offender should be taken into account at this point to obtain a complete understanding of all consequences.

Finally, to understand the offence and the offender and to impose a fair sentence, one needs to comprehend the context in which the offender committed the offence. We differentiate three different types of contexts: material, formal and societal. The material context relates to the circumstances under which the offender committed the offence and either aggravates or mitigates the offender's blameworthiness. Misuse of the victim's trust and domestic violence preceding a murder in cold blood by an abuser are examples of such material contexts. The formal context is linked solely to criminal proceedings and especially its (undue) length. If – by no fault of the offender – the criminal proceedings were too long, a court must reduce the sentence. Finally, the social context – a category typically not previewed by the law – might also influence what sentence a judge will impose; thefts committed during riots might lead judges to impose more severe sentences than comparable thefts at other times.

However, the division of factors into several groups which together form a story, while helpful for understanding the complexity of sentencing, is insufficient to aid judges in a principled decision on what sentence they should impose and in explaining why they should choose such a sentence. An unstructured process of selecting a sentence and providing reasoning for it does not sufficiently prevent deficiencies that might occur due to the large number of factors that judges have to consider. The shortcomings are mainly the following three:

- *Non-consideration of a factor*: If considered factors are not enumerated, judges might omit factors which they ought to have considered and include factors which should not influence the sentence imposition. To omit considering a factor is simple: if there is a limited time to sentence an offender and many factors to consider, judges might quickly pay attention to only selected factors. If justification is not adequately structured, it might be impossible to check and possibly correct a consideration of an improper factor; for example, the authors have experienced anecdotally judges mentioning that, if a defendant does not wear a button-up shirt at the hearing, they impose a significantly longer prison sentence, although such factor should be (virtually) irrelevant to sentencing. As reason-giving is unstructured, they get away with it.
- *Lack of specification of the factor*: A variation of non-consideration of a factor is if a judge considers a factor (e.g., mentions "a criminal history") but does not discuss the significance which the factor acquires in the present case. In these situations, the value of a general mention of such factor is low, due to the lack of knowledge about its specificity. On the contrary, suppose a judge specifies a factor; in this case, its source will also typically be recognisable to the defendant and the prosecution, enabling them to question the source or the standard of proof and provide additional evidence.
- *Insufficient determination of the importance of individual factors and the final decision*: Upon deciding and explaining what influenced the imposition of a sentence, a judge can easily assign a particular factor an improper role, which is either too large or too small. For example, the offender's behaviour during the hearing – such as the perceived sincerity of an apology – might be overestimated if judges experience it just before deciding on the sentence. Similarly, some have argued that previous convictions play too large a role in sentencing (Frase & Roberts, 2019). Unless sentencing and reason-giving are structured through an explanation of the role of individual factors in reaching the final decision, the role of individual factors might be over- or underappreciated.

These shortcomings (and briefly outlined solutions) should not come as any surprise to a legal professional – or to a poker player. Just as other players can understand each other's decisions only upon showdown or when playing with an open hand, a sentencing decision can only be understood when judges present and specify factors influencing the sentence imposition. Each card is of a specific type and carries a certain value; both these kinds of information need to be revealed. It is of little significance to know that a particular card is a spade, just as it is of little significance to know when a judge has considered an offender's criminal history; players typically demand to know additional details, such as the value of the card or the details of previous convictions.

Finally, cards must be appropriately combined according to their type and values to achieve an outcome. Similarly, unless the factors are combined and weighted, a resulting sentence will not persuade the spectators (and will possibly be a wrong one). Once we realise these shortcomings, we can focus on the solutions.

Three stages of reasoning

In this section, we develop three stages of reasoning – identification, evaluation and weighing – corresponding to the three previously discussed problems. While sentencing scholarship has never specifically discussed these three stages, they are typical of how lawyers think and are employed by continental criminal judges when deciding on guilt. It would be unimaginable for a continental judge to find an offender guilty and justify that they have "taken into account all pieces of evidence, both individually and together, especially those presented by the witnesses, and considered all incriminating and exculpating evidence." Such a general phrase would not satisfy anyone. Judges would first describe individual types of evidence – not in general terms but concerning specific facts. Then, they would mention whether these pieces of evidence incriminate or liberate the offender and how strong the evidence which they present is (in other words, how persuasive it is). Finally, judges would weigh all incriminating and liberating evidence. If they conclude that incriminating evidence crosses a threshold of being beyond reasonable doubt, they explain their reasons for it by contrasting different kinds of evidence in combination with and against each other. Such an approach would greatly benefit sentence justifications as well.

Identification and specification

First, judges must *identify* the factors requiring consideration and how they are *specified*. This should ensure that judges properly identify all factors influencing the sentencing decision. This allows the court to build solid foundations for constructing the sentence. At this point, no decision about the influence of a factor needs to be made, as even factors that will not influence the decision might be identified and specified. For example, a judge might initially identify and specify an expression of remorse by the offender, but later they might conclude that this should play only a minor role since it was deemed insincere. For such a decision to be possible, the judge needs to note that remorse was expressed and how it was expressed (e.g., the defendant sent a letter to the court via an attorney).

There is empirical evidence showing the importance of the specification of individual factors. Psychological literature suggests that the more we explain our decisions, the better we identify subtle differences between cases (Lombrozo, 2012). Given that one of the goals of sentencing is to impose a fair individualised sentence, identifying the subtle differences between cases is of high importance. The specification should thus foster individualisation. Additionally, people are less punitive when presented with a specific case compared with when they are asked about their general attitude towards sanctions' level of punitiveness (de Keijser et al., 2007; Diamond & Stalans, 1989; Hough & Roberts, 1999; Kuhn, 2002; St Amand & Zamble, 2001). If it is because one cannot "imagine" a human being behind the mask of the offender, specification might help in this respect.

Judges should be guided to consider all factors via a checklist, while being allowed to consider factors that the checklist does not preview. Such a checklist could be developed based on the requirements of individual penal codes and codes of criminal procedure and sentencing scholarship. Anecdotal evidence collected by one of the authors suggests the essential role such a checklist could play; upon presenting it to an experienced prosecutor at training and requiring him to provide reasoning based on it, he mentioned that he would not have considered half of the factors were it not for the checklist.

The checklist should then guide judges to specify forms of the factors relevant to the tried case. All factors should be specified either in full or at least partially while referring to an earlier part of the verdict (a complete reference might require more clarity about the content of a factor). For example, if a court refers to the "circumstances of the offender," the "seriousness of the offence" or the "egregious motive" and simply refers to earlier parts of the decision, readers (and possibly even judges) might not understand the content. Specifying a factor would further enable a discussion concerning whether the factor has been properly individualised and whether the underlying evidence is sufficient. Both the defendant and the prosecution could object to the specification and present additional evidence.

It would thus be insufficient for a judge to mention both broad categories of factors (e.g., "the nature of the offence was considered") and an unspecified factor ("the offender's criminal history was considered"). A specific elaboration of all applicable factors is needed. Otherwise, it is unclear whether judges have considered all applicable factors and whether the court gathered sufficient evidence to impose a principled sentence.

Identification and specification are necessary for everyone who is broadly interested in sentencing. A judge could make sure that he or she has not forgotten to consider any factor and has not considered factors which one should not take into account; identification and specification would further enable judges to decide on their role during the following steps. Parties would see what factors a court considered and how it specified them, allowing parties to question whether additional factors should be considered and to provide new evidence that would lead to a different specification of a factor. For the criminal justice system, identification and specification are essential requirements for developing sentencing principles. Unless the factors are specified, there cannot be any debate about what role they should play. Finally, the public will get an option to understand the judge; without identification and specification, one simply needs to believe that judges have considered all factors (Hutton, 2015). While having trust in judges is important, it is better if such trust is based on facts.

Measuring

Once a factor is identified and specified, the judge has to conclude how its presence influences the sentence. Different factors impact sentencing differently according to their specification, so the judge needs to be clear about the influence of different factors in a particular case. First, a judge needs to specify whether a factor *benefits the offender or puts them at a disadvantage.* While the direction would typically be evident, it will not always be. For example, whether the offender committed the offence under influence can be either aggravating or mitigating depending on the circumstances in question (Lightowlers et al., 2022).

Second, a judge should decide on the *approximate strength of the factor*. While it would be improper and futile to direct judges to quantify the strength of individual factors, mentioning whether the factor should have a low, medium or high effect on the sentence is necessary. One aggravating circumstance may have a more substantial impact than four mitigating ones, so an approximate evaluation of the influence is required to move to the next step (the *weighing of all factors*). For example, the guilty plea of a person caught while driving under the influence (there being irrefutable evidence) will very likely influence the sentence differently than a guilty plea in a complex white-collar crime case. Finally, various factors might influence different decisions throughout the sentencing process. For example, some should influence the imposition of incapacitative measures but do not necessarily influence the "penal value" of the offence. Judges should thus clarify what part of the imposed sentence is influenced by the factor. In the final chapter, we elaborate on the consideration of specific factors at specific points in the process of sentence imposition.

Specifying the importance of a factor also serves as a safeguard against judges who would provide a long list of factors which they have (allegedly) taken into account but who use it only to escape appellate review. This was the approach of Swiss and German courts during the 1980s and 1990s (Killias, 1994). Once the courts were required to mention each factor's role, appellate courts could more easily question the first-level courts' conclusions and counter their claims of considering too many factors, while doing so only formally.

Mentioning the factor's direction and strength will allow the court to apply sentencing principles in a specific context, further advancing principled sentencing. Considering the role of an individual factor also enables better consideration of all factors in the next step; without it, the final imposition of a sentence would be too burdensome. For other audiences – the parties, the criminal justice system, and the public – such mentions enable discussion and clearer understanding of the decision. These explanations are also necessary for policy purposes. Suppose that sentencing systems want to elaborate the role which different forms of various factors should play in sentencing. In that case, there is no other practical way than to require judges to specify each factor and to express the role which each factor should play, thereby allowing appellate courts to rule on them.

Weighing

The final step consists in declaring a sentence by combining all the factors. The formulation of each factor's role is insufficient (albeit conducive to imposing a final sentence), as judges need to consider all factors together. Therefore, to explicitly weigh all factors and arrive at a sentence is necessary. Otherwise, the decisions are not understandable and replicable and remain – to some extent – a black box. "Considering all factors mentioned above, the court has decided to impose a sentence XY" is a phrase too familiar to many continental lawyers; it does not clarify why a judge has reached the specific decision in any way.

In conducting the weighing phase, the court should explain why a specific sentence is appropriate given all the factors present in the case. Since sentencing decision is still very complex – one has to impose the main and auxiliary sentences, each of which follows a different sentencing rationale – weighing needs to relate to individual decisions judges make when sentencing. Weighing should take place for individual sentencing steps – such as the ones outlined in the final chapter – in order to make the final decision more structured and more accessible.

Only explicitly weighing all factors can ensure that the judge is making a principled decision. Various factors will acquire different forms, and their combination would be (to some extent) unique in every case. Weighing leads to a principled consideration of the specific combination. Moreover, it enables the parties and the public to properly review the mental process undertaken by the judge and, as a result, understand the complexity behind the decision.

Benefits of reasoning structured in three stages

The three stages of reasoning will enable judges to achieve both individualised and principled sentences. The sentences will be individualised, since the three stages stress that all factors need to be considered and that all factors need to be specified (preferably based on sufficient evidence). The sentences will also be principled, because, especially within the second and third stages, this approach requires explicit decisions about the influence of individual factors and various forms which they might acquire on a sentence. Once these decisions are made explicit and once appellate and supreme courts review them, a proper sentencing jurisprudence might develop.

If taken seriously by all criminal justice actors, the three stages can improve the quality of sentencing outcomes and process. We envision that prosecutors could recommend sentences while identifying all relevant factors, specifying them, and mentioning whether they benefit the defendant or are to his or her disadvantage, what role they play and how the prosecution has weighted them all together. Defendants could also either prepare a similar document or question only single elements or individual reasoning decisions in the prosecution. In such a way, the discussion concerning individual factors, the evidence supporting them and their role would already occur in front of the first-level court.

Upon sentencing, a judge would either (partially) accept the individual parties' arguments or provide their assessment of the case and impose a sentence. Such a decision could be a foundation for principled appeals which claim that first-level courts should or should not have considered certain factors and that they should play a different role. Appellate courts could simply review the steps taken by the first-level courts, rule on factual questions and focus on the interpretation of principles. Supreme courts could review the sentencing principles at a more theoretical level, leading to an elaboration of these principles.

While the three stages strongly contribute to principled decision-making and reasoning, they alone might not be sufficient to result in structured decision-making, although they can serve as a necessary component. The sentencing decision requires the additional structuring of individual sub-decisions forming a sentence. Some factors primarily influence the sub-decision whether to incarcerate the offender or not, others are important for defining the offence's seriousness level (and thus the extent of the penalty), and others might be essential only for the sub-decision on an imposition of incapacitative and rehabilitative sanctions and measures. The sentencing process should, thus, be further subdivided to make gradually separate sub-decisions on sentences at different phases. These phases should reflect the sentencing rationales of individual systems. Especially systems which emphasise proportionality as a primary sentencing rationale (or which are at least ascribed to a limited retributivist approach) require the division of the sentencing process into several steps. We provide a specific example in the final chapter.

Conclusion

Judges have rarely – and in most countries, never – been provided with guidance on how they should provide reasons for the sentences they impose. Given that most countries do not operate strict sentencing guidelines (the United States being an exception), one can expect the judges' decision-making to include shortcomings in both making the decision and providing the reasoning for it. Specifically, we can expect them to either omit factors which they should consider or to consider factors that should never play a role. Additionally, even if they consider a type of factor, they might misinterpret the form acquired in the specific case. Judges might also try to evade the control of appellate courts by enumerating various factors without assigning them a level of importance and by not considering them all together, leading to the imposed sentence being unreviewable.

Most judges want to do their job correctly, and they want to impose just and consistent sentences. The three stages developed in this chapter aim to ensure precisely that. Principled and individualised sentencing is unimaginable without identifying and specifying factors, their evaluation and their weighing. The appeal of this approach is that judges retain the level of discretion they wield, while ensuring a more structured and accountable decision.

Such an approach will likely result in sentencing decisions taking longer than a few minutes to be both taken and written. Such investment is, in our view, helpful and necessary. Sentencing consists in judges making the most critical decisions which a state can take concerning individual persons and their rights. While a decision on guilt is an essential prerequisite, the sentence influences one's life. It cannot be made lightly and must be properly reasoned and explained.

At the same time, the time constraints which judges face in their everyday decision-making need to be acknowledged and, if possible, offset. Thus, judges should be presented with something other than a theoretical book chapter on sentencing and reason-giving for imposed sentences. Instead, they should be provided with a specific and easy form which they might fill in to fulfil the requirement of providing proper reasoning for sentences. Each country needs to prepare its own documentation; we supply an example suitable for one country in the final chapter. Such forms should, however, fulfil the following general principles:

- The form should include a list of the most common factors for judges to consider, divided according to different sub-groups, especially if national legislation enumerates factors that may or have to be considered. The form should enable the inclusion of factors other than the anticipated ones.
- The form should provide an opportunity to specify each factor, and judges should be required to specify all factors applicable to the case.
- For every applicable factor, it should be mentioned whether a factor is in favour or to the disadvantage of an offender (or whether it does not play any role). Judges should further specify the approximate importance of each factor.
- The weighing of individual factors in reaching a decision should be made explicit.

Reasoning which fulfils these principles will lead in individual cases to an individualised and principled sentencing decision and an understandable decision. It may also contribute to a general system of more principled sentencing based on jurisprudence and discussions (in academia and in legal practice) as a result of this jurisprudence.

4 Sentence justification in first-level courts in post-communist Europe

Jakub Drápal, Augustina Bolocan-Holban, Jaan Ginter, Mojca Plesničar, Kristýna Tomšů, and Mihaela Vidaicu

Introduction

Reason-giving is at present the only manifestation of the court's use of sentencing discretion in post-communist countries. The defendant, the victim, the prosecutor, the appellate court, or the public are not provided with other opportunities to understand why courts impose particular sentences (such as sentencing guidelines). Given the importance of accountability and transparency (see Chapter 2), we study the reasons given for sentences in different parts of post-communist Europe: Czechia, Estonia, Moldova, Slovakia and Slovenia. This list includes both EU and non-EU countries, as well as countries which belong or have belonged to the former Warsaw Pact, Yugoslavia and CCCP. This study substantially enlarges the scarce scholarship on sentencing in this region, as criminologists in these countries have not yet studied to what extent courts are accountable for decisions they make. Without such evidence, discussion on sentencing is difficult to conduct, yet such discussions are necessary given the recently identified high levels of sentencing disparities and the virtually non-existent discussion over how sentencing discretion should be structured (Drápal & Plesničar, 2023) in this region.

We study the reasons given for sentences from different perspectives – legal, criminological and societal – and focus on why and with what aims courts impose and communicate sentences. A valuable feature of this study is that we study reason-giving across five countries; this research is the first comparative study focusing on reason-giving which employs this methodology. Our study thus paints a complex picture of reason-giving in post-communist Europe.

The chapter first provides an overview of the sentencing framework, emphasising rules about reason-giving. We then discuss the employed method and the samples analysed. Most of our attention is devoted to the presentation of our results. First, we discuss the general level of reasoning

DOI: 10.4324/9781003470670-4

on a country-by-country basis. Next, we discuss Schuyt's three stages of reason-giving (see Chapter 3) to ascertain to what extent others might reproduce judicial decisions given the sentence justification alone. We then focus on sentencing rationales expressed in different sentencing decisions and consider whether courts mention necessary corresponding factors. Lastly, we focus on storytelling and to what extent courts mention individual aspects of a story in their decisions. We close the chapter by discussing the take-away message from the results, drawing conclusions about the level of accountability in post-communist countries and discussing possible improvements.

Sentencing systems: similarities and differences

A practice of reason-giving can be adequately understood only with the knowledge of relevant sentencing systems and the rules governing reason-giving. Thus, we first provide a general overview of the rules, emphasising similarities and differences across individual countries. Then, we present rules governing reason-giving in individual countries, exceptions to them and the frequency of reason-giving.

General sentencing framework

Post-communist European countries typically place a strong emphasis on individualisation (Plesničar, 2013). This "every-case-is-unique" approach (Tata, 2020) is emphasised more than in other European countries. There are important historical and societal reasons for this. One of them is the lack of proper sentencing debates in the 1970s and 1980s as a result of underfunding in the social sciences, which were in some countries completely under the influence of communist ideology, and no or minimal empirical research on sentencing disparities was being carried out (see Drápal & Plesničar (2023) for elaboration of these issues and those discussed in this section).

The criminal code typically grants judges and prosecutors[1] broad discretion without providing them with principles sufficiently structuring it. Judges impose sentences within relatively wide sentencing ranges, and criminal codes present fundamental general principles regarding sentencing multiple and repeat offenders and a list of aggravating and mitigating factors. After that, however, judges must go on their own; in most post-communist countries, no textbook or sentencing training exists. Their only possible anchoring point is "how it was always done at this court," which is communicated

1 In some countries, prosecutors recommend sentences, so the same rules apply to them as to judges. From now on, we will talk only about judges. However, generally, the same arguments apply to prosecutors as well.

by their colleagues, as sentence orientations or guidelines are non-existent (except for the case of Moldova). The only institution that controls and guides first-level judges are appellate courts, as supreme courts do not rule on sentencing principles (except for the case of Estonia). Additionally, even appellate courts do not provide sufficient guidance (see Chapter 5). Judges are thus given significant discretion without proper guidance (Drápal & Plesničar, 2023).

Reason-giving is especially important in systems with such broad discretion since no-one can understand why a court made a particular decision without reasoning. The emphasis placed on individualisation should – theoretically – also lead judges to justify their decisions in detail, as the individual features of the case need to be mentioned to demonstrate the case's individuality. Reason-giving should, thus, play a crucial role in the sentencing process.

Practically, proper reason-giving is challenging as it is difficult to achieve principled sentencing; judges have little guidance on what to do, making it difficult to explain why they did something. Both substantive guidance (what principles to consider and how they should influence the decision) and procedural guidance (how a sentencing procedure, including reason provision, should look) are missing. Judges are thus faced with a difficult task; reason-giving is essential but burdensome. They thus have to choose between the time-consuming and difficult task of explaining how they used the discretion, or they might collectively (and tacitly) choose to ignore the task of true reason-giving. If most judges ignore this requirement, an appellate court would likely not criticise an individual judge for ignoring it, as otherwise, appellate courts would have to interfere very frequently. Anecdotal evidence has suggested that judges – both first-level and in appellate courts – tend to take the easy way out.

The pragmatic approach of not providing reasons for imposed sentences has not been challenged by researchers or other institutions for a long time. Previous empirical research on reason-giving was either scarce or non-existent. In Estonia, for example, reasons given for imposed sentences were studied primarily for the cases of murder and theft. Before 1989, the Czechoslovak Supreme Court regularly analysed courts' reason-giving in Czechoslovakia and typically found the extent of reason-giving to be insufficient. However, the Court did not use any scientific method in its reason-giving procedures; its approach was the typical legal method of "reading and making conclusions." Apart from such scarce empirical research, criminal lawyers have sometimes made claims about poor reasoning quality. However, their arguments were never adequately substantiated by empirical research, enabling others to downplay them as the opinions of individuals. Low levels of reasoning were thus long suspected but never proven.

Requirements regarding reasoning and frequency of reason-giving

The examined countries have similar rules regarding reason-giving, although they differ to some extent regarding (i) when a court can issue a decision without providing reasons for it, and (ii) what proportion of decisions includes reasoning. In what follows, we will thus discuss in detail the rules governing reason-giving in individual countries and the frequency with which judges provide reasons for sentences in individual countries.

Every *Czech* judgment should include reasoning. There are, however, three main exceptions to this rule. The most important one is that it relates only to judgments but not to penal orders. A penal order is a simplified procedure that includes neither written nor oral reasoning and consists of a letter outlining the behaviour, legal classification and sentence. Between 2016 and 2018, courts sentenced 57.2% of all offenders via a penal order. When a court decides by a judgment, reasons are given, at least in oral form. Courts only provide written reasoning if neither party waives their right to an appeal; if waived, the court prepares only a simplified verdict without reasoning. A slightly underestimated valuation of simplified verdicts is 18.2%.[2] Thirdly, judges do not provide reasoning in cases of plea bargaining, although these cases are rare before 2020. This results in 24.6% of offenders being given a written verdict (approximately 14,475 per year). The form of reasoning is not specified, although the Code of Criminal Procedure includes a long list of factors that should be mentioned when providing reasoning for imposed sentences and directs courts to provide specific reasoning why a non-custodial sentence could not be imposed if the court imposes a custodial sentence (s. 125/1). Until 2020, neither jurisprudence nor academia provided guidance on how to justify imposed sentences.

Estonian courts do not have to provide reasoning following plea bargaining (in 2017, 4,738 out of 6,802 criminal cases) and they give only limited reasons following summary proceedings (172 cases). When either abridged proceedings (the court hears no witnesses and decides only based on case file, 1,455 cases) or complete proceedings (437 cases) occur, judges provide oral reasons and written reasoning only when an appeal is filed. In 2017, appeals were filed in 259 cases against general proceedings, 188 cases against abridged proceedings and 91 cases against plea-bargaining proceedings. The law does not prescribe what exactly reason-giving should look like but specifies that a court should provide additional reasoning when incarcerating an offender.

Moldovian courts must provide written reasons in all their decisions, even when a decision results from plea bargaining or a simplified verdict is issued. Theoretically, 100% of cases should include written reasoning, but,

2 Proportion of decisions acquiring legal force on the same day when imposed.

in practice, judges do not often provide reasons for imposed sentences following simplified procedures such as plea bargaining. Reasons given for sentences direct judges to carefully consider whether incarceration is necessary; if a non-suspended prison sentence is imposed, judges should explain why other main punishments were not appropriate, and in doing so, judges should consider especially offence harmfulness and the offender's personality. Jurisprudence and judicial training mention sentence reasoning but do not elaborate on it in detail.

Although the general rule holds that *Slovak* verdicts should include written reasoning, it provides the same three main avenues for how judges might evade it as in Czechia: (i) imposition of a penal order, (ii) parties waiving their rights to an appeal leading to a simplified verdict and (iii) plea bargaining. A penal order is imposed in 68% of cases, and, out of the remaining verdicts, approximately 29.5% contain written reasoning. 9.4% of offenders thus receive written reasons for the sentence imposed by a court. Regarding the form of reasons given for sentences, the Slovak Penal Code only specifies that there should be reasoning and does not specify what it should include; it is not elaborated in detail by jurisprudence or academia.

Giving reasons in all cases in *Slovenia* is generally required, but there is also a notable exception. If none of the parties announces an appeal, reasons only need to be given if the court passes a non-suspended prison sentence. In cases which are decided by a penal order, only very general reasoning is provided (which does not extend beyond the prosecution's charges). In cases decided via plea bargaining or as a result of a guilty plea at a pre-trial hearing, the reasoning could, in theory, be substantial but is typically still very general. In 2017–2018, courts provided such general reasoning in 70.1% of cases. In an additional 11.7% of cases, no written reasons were given (only oral reasons were provided) as an appeal was not announced; in the remaining 18.1% of cases, reasons for the imposed sentences were given since an appeal was announced. In such cases, judges are directed to explain what factors they considered upon sentencing and to provide specific reasoning for certain decisions (e.g., imposing a sentence below the minimum sentencing range or imposing a suspended prison sentence). Neither laws, jurisprudence nor academia advise judges on how to provide better sentence reasoning.

Across the five examined countries, the consensus is that exceptions are the rule; decisions including written reasoning are less and less common, but theoretically they are still considered the rule (with Moldova not recognising any exception, but only on paper; in practice, exceptions exist in Moldova). While efficiency is important, exceptions emphasise the low attention paid to sentencing; following a penal order, a plea-agreement decision or when parties did not file an appeal or waived their rights to file an appeal, no written reasoning is required. We consider the appropriateness of these exceptions in the later discussion.

Not surprisingly, the most reasoned decisions per capita (Table 4.1) are in Moldova, which requires virtually all decisions to include reasoning. In the most studied countries – Estonia, Slovakia and Slovenia – there are few reasoned decisions per 100,000 inhabitants (and thus per judge). For example, Slovakia has approximately 800 district judges, one third of which are criminal judges, meaning that a Slovak criminal judge provides written reasoning for sentences he or she imposes less than once a month. One might ask whether such frequency is sufficient to become an expert in reason-giving. This low frequency is at least partly the result of the introduction of limitations on when written reasoning should be provided since 1989/1991 (in the cases of Czechia, Slovakia and Slovenia) and the introduction and wide use of penal orders and guilty pleas (in the cases of Slovakia and Slovenia). Czechia rests between the two camps, partly because a court prepares a simplified verdict if parties do not waive their right to an appeal (defendants have to waive it explicitly), compared with Estonia and Slovenia, where written reasons for sentences are given only when an appeal is announced or filed (defendants have to file it explicitly).

In these circumstances, we would expect courts to provide a reasoning of low quality. Judges are given broad discretion and low guidance, making a principled decision difficult and accountability burdensome. Only the rhetoric of individualisation contributes to the decision; if every case is different and one cannot compare sentences imposed in different cases (Drápal & Plesničar, 2023), is it necessary to discuss precisely which factors played what role? Additionally, both the high and low frequency of requiring reason-giving might be problematic. We would expect both widespread and rare provision of reasons to contribute to a low quality of given reasons due to either time pressure or difficulties in learning the craft. Therefore, we would expect the best reasoning to occur in systems where reason-giving is common but is not

Table 4.1 Reasoned decisions in individual countries

Country	*Number of reasoned cases per year*	*Reasoned decisions per 100,000 inhabitants*
Czechia	14,475	137
Estonia	614	47
Moldova	7,667	278
Slovakia	1,992	37
Slovenia	1,224	59

Note: Regarding the population for Moldova, we exclude Transnistria. The analysed period is the following: Moldova 2016–2017; Czechia 2016–2018; Estonia 2017; Slovenia 2017–2018; Slovakia 2018.

required in every case and in systems where judges provide reasons but are afforded sufficient time.

Method: content analysis

Content analysis is the preferred method of studying the frequency of factors occurring in court decisions (Hall & Wright, 2008). According to this approach, the researcher prepares a coding manual that specifies the variables of interest and values they might acquire and explains the variables and the values. Ideally, two or more researchers code each decision, so that their consistency can be examined. We followed these best practices, yet unfortunately there were insufficient funds to code the decisions by two or more researchers; therefore, only one researcher coded each decision. Additionally, although all researchers followed the same manual and protocol, discussed the realisation of content analysis generally and concerning specific issues and were provided with examples of good practice, there was no empirical check whether the coders in individual countries were coding decisions similarly. Thus, every researcher could have coded the same decision partially differently, which would limit the possibility of comparing the results across countries. We thus primarily display results by country.

Different researchers coded decisions from their countries, except for one person who coded both the Czech and Slovak decisions. The decisions were coded by Kristýna Tomšů (Czechia and Slovakia), Jaan Ginter (Estonia), Mojca Plesničar (Slovenia, being aided by Lora Briški and Marko Balažic) and Mihaela Vidaicu (Moldova, being aided by Augustina Bolocan-Holban and Ecaterina Vornicescu). The coding of the decisions by researchers from one country might introduce a certain level of bias. Nevertheless, this could not have been realistically avoided given the lack of coders who speak Czech, Slovak, Estonian, Romanian and Slovenian. Jakub Drápal prepared the coding manual and resolved any issues. The coding was conducted on the same platform, JotForm, except for the case of the Czech Republic, which was coded on a different platform (MS Excel) using the same coding manual.

After recording basic information about the offence (offence type, sentencing ranges and imposed sentences), we first recorded the extent of reasoning: whether there was none, only a general one (such as a phrase "concerning the seriousness of the crime and the person of the offender, the court has imposed a following sentence") or a specific one. Then, we studied weighing, that is, its presence and its summary, and sentencing aims (a choice was given between specific deterrence, incapacitation, rehabilitation, general deterrence, retribution and a possible other aim). We recorded the length of the decision, the specific reasoning of the case and whether the case was presented as a story; an open-ended question was asked so that the story could be succinctly reproduced.

We then directed the attention towards individual reasons (factors). Firstly, a researcher chose a factor type from 12 possibilities with an enabled write-in. Out of these, we formed the following five categories that contained the following factors: (i) offence related – the effect of the crime (harm), seriousness of the act, intent/aim of the offender, committed under the influence of/in connection with drugs, attempt/preparation, multiple offences; (ii) life prior to sentencing – offending history and a write-in way of life so far, (iii) personal circumstances; (iv) after commission – remorse, reparation of damages by the offender, guilt admission and cooperation with the authorities and write-in behaviour after committal; and (v) other – cause of crime (what was the driving force) and write-ins time passed, effects from punishment for the offender, cause of crime and context. We then recorded in relation to what decision the court mentioned this factor, with the options being as follows: no specification, type of sanction, length of sanction, modality of sanction (suspended/non-suspended), several of the above and an enabled write-in option (write-ins included judicial economy, conduct of the offender and defendant's character). If the reason was related to a specific sentence, we registered it according to what sentence type the court mentioned.

We then inquired about the quality of the factor: whether it was specified or not – the specification required an explanation of what happened in an individual case; to what one of the five story questions the factor related (see Chapter 3); whether the factor was (implicitly or explicitly) considered as mitigating or aggravating or whether it was not mentioned (a write-in option was enabled); and its importance. We distinguished decisive, medium and low levels of importance (not mentioned and a write-in option were also enabled). Finally, we recorded a full or shortened text of the reason and anything else worth mentioning.

Samples

To provide a complex and reliable perspective on the justification of sentences imposed across the region, we studied representative samples of decisions from different parts of post-communist Europe. The examined countries include former Warsaw Pact countries (the Czech Republic and Slovakia), the former Yugoslavia (Slovenia) and the former CCCP (Estonia and Moldova). The analysed decisions should thus reflect closely the quality of reason-giving in the five examined countries, despite some regional limitations.

The Czech sample consisted of 366 reasoned decisions, representative of decisions taken by district courts in 2016. District courts deal with 98% of cases; they do not deal with the most serious ones (this role is assigned to regional courts, which were later analysed separately; see Forman (2023)). We randomly selected this sample, with stratification at the district court level.

The Estonian sample consisted of 268 decisions. The sample included all judgements with full reasons made by the Estonian courts of first instance in criminal cases of adult persons between 22 April 2016 and 27 February 2019, for which there was a link to the text of the judgment on the Riigi Teataja website.

The Moldovian sample consisted of 300 decisions made in 2018, randomly chosen to reflect the jurisprudence of all 15 courts across the country. We randomly generated the combination of a date and a court and used the courts' portal (www.instante.justice.md) to identify the decisions based on the issue date and the court name. In the case that no decision was made on the selected date, we chose a decision made in the same month close to the randomly chosen date. We excluded guilty pleas as they generally did not include any reasons, resulting in 202 analysable decisions.

The Slovak sample consisted of 204 reasoned decisions. Originally, we randomly chose 692 decisions from the official website of the Slovak Ministry of Justice, containing almost complete decisions made in 2018. The simplified verdicts and guilty pleas were excluded.

The Slovenian sample consisted of a randomly chosen total of 587 decisions from 6 courts (3 local and 3 district courts) that were made in 2019 (every 10th decision was selected). The sample included decisions in which the final decision was either an acquittal or other decisions that did not carry a sentence, which were omitted from the analysis of sentencing reasoning; this resulted in a final number of 400 decisions. We have excluded those that did not include any reasoning due to the decision being taken via penal order, as a result of a guilty plea or a simplified verdict being issued. This resulted in 236 decisions.

Results

The presentation of the results reflects different perspectives on reason-giving – legal, criminological and societal – to paint a complex picture. Firstly, we are interested in the overall picture of reasoning. The easiest way for a judge to conclude a case is to provide general reasoning: the copy-pasted sentence "All factors relating to the offence and to the offender were considered both individually and in combination with each other" (or its slightly prolonged version) might impress the parties (especially if courts use more erudite words), but in effect does not carry any message. It seems that every country has a version of such a phrase. We are thus interested in how often courts provide such general reasoning and how often better versions of reason-giving appear.

Secondly, we focus on evaluating the three stages of reason-giving, as outlined in Chapter 3. We specifically want to investigate the extent to which factors are specified, how often judges state factors' importance and direction and how often weighing takes place. Thirdly, we follow the sentencing scholarship which emphasises the role that sentencing rationales (aims) play in sentencing decisions. We go beyond a simple description of citing the frequency of mentioned sentencing aims and study the extent to which judges consider factors related to the sentencing aim they mention. It is, for example, impossible to mention retribution/proportionality as a sentencing aim and omit discussion of harm and offence seriousness. Therefore, we analyse whether mentioning a specific sentencing aim is reflected in discussing factors relating to the sentencing aim. Finally, we return to another aspect described in Chapter 3: storytelling. We describe to what extent courts present reasoning as a story and what questions sentencers answer most commonly.

The general level of reasoning

An overall insight into how judges justify imposed sentences can be best achieved by dividing decisions into categories ranging from no reasoning to elaborated reasoning processes. Properly elaborated decisions should (i) mention individual factors, (ii) specify them, (iii) discuss how much they influenced the decision and in what direction, and (iv) consider how factors were weighed. We have divided court decisions into six categories according to the extent to which they fulfil these criteria:

1. There were no reasons related to the sentence.
2. Only general reasoning was given, but no individual factor was mentioned.
3. At least one factor was mentioned, but not even one was specified in relation to the individual case and offender.
4. At least one factor was specified in relation to the individual case and/or offender. However, its direction (such as aggravating or mitigating) and importance (how much it influenced the sentence imposition) were not mentioned.
5. At least one factor was specified and its direction and importance were mentioned, but all factors were not weighed.
6. At least one factor was specified, direction and importance were mentioned and all factors were weighed.

Overall, very few decisions fulfil all four requirements (i.e., and reach category 6), as Figure 4.1 suggests. In Estonia, Moldova and Slovenia, such decisions were infrequent. They were more common in Czechia and Slovakia but always represented no more than an important minority of cases. In some countries, it is thus impossible to understand (by recreating) why judges imposed particular sentences in almost all cases, while in other countries it is impossible to do so for a large majority of cases. Simply put, the level of reasoning is poor.

While we are aware of the methodological issues limiting the possibility of comparing results from individual countries, there is evidence suggesting that the approach of individual countries differs. Moldovan judges provide

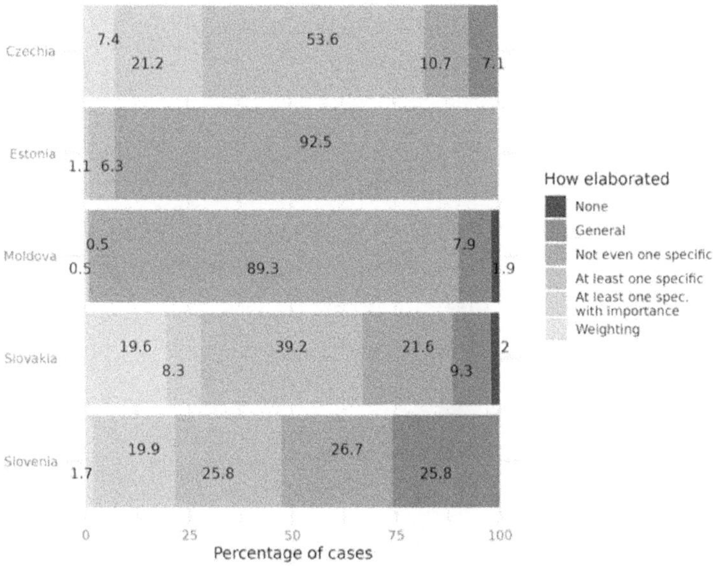

Figure 4.1 Elaboration of decisions per country

Note: N = 1286 decisions.

the least information; most decisions do not include even one specified factor. Those in-betweens are Slovenia and Estonia. The Slovenian courts provide only general reasoning in one quarter of cases. The Estonian courts often specify individual factors but rarely mention their importance or weigh them against each other. Slovakia and Czechia were among the best, with Czechia being ahead. Nevertheless, in the land of the blind, the one-eyed man is king.

Evaluation of the three stages of reason-giving

We next study the three stages of reasoning, as defined in Chapter 3. These are (i) specification of a factor, (ii) discussion of the importance of each factor and the direction in which it influences a decision and (iii) weighing of all the factors. In doing so, we excluded decisions that did not mention at least one factor (those with labels "None" or "General" in Figure 4.1), resulting in 1,155 decisions containing 3,461 factors.

First, we examine how many factors were specified and how many factors one decision typically mentions. Figure 4.2 suggests that the trends differ by country: in Estonia and Moldova, courts typically mention 1–3

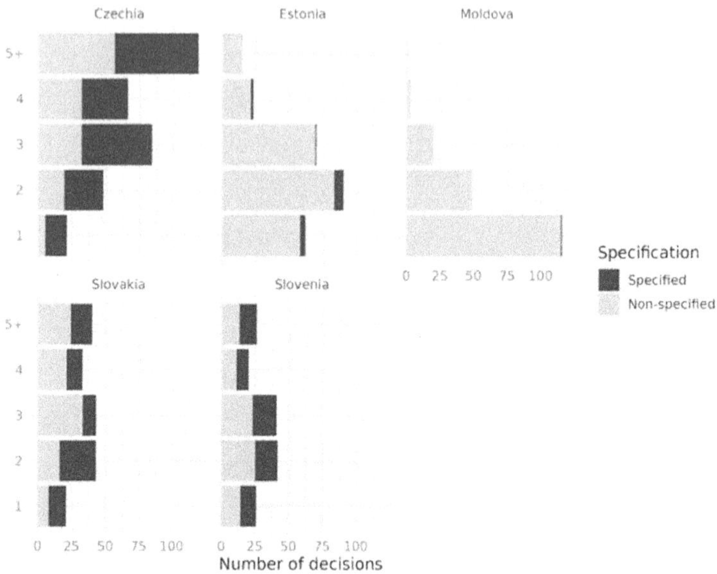

Figure 4.2 Number of factors by specification and country

Note: N = 1122 decisions.

factors (with virtually all of them being not specified); in Slovenia and Slovakia, courts typically include 2–3 factors per decision (with the majority being not specified) and in Czechia 3–5+ factors were included, with a slight majority being specified. This suggests that individual factors are not sufficiently specified and do not provide an opportunity to understand what the factor is supposed to represent; a simple reference to previous convictions or offence seriousness does not enable readers to understand the factor. The basic requirement to achieve an individualised sentence is lacking; if factors are not specified, no-one can discuss whether its ensuing use and role is appropriate.

The frequency of individual factors, the level of their specification and their use in individual countries is displayed in Table 4.2. The most common factors are offending history, personal circumstances and cooperation with authorities; other frequently mentioned factors are harm, seriousness, remorse, multiple offending and the way of life prior to the committal of an offence. This suggests that – at least in their reasoning – judges place a higher emphasis on factors related to consequentialist (utilitarian) sentencing aims rather than to proportionality-based aims. This is especially true in Slovakia

Table 4.2 Percentage of mentioned factors out of all decisions and percentage of specification of such factors

	Czechia	*Estonia*	*Moldova*	*Slovakia*	*Slovenia*
Harm	40% (55%)	38% (5%)	3% (0%)	9% (44%)	35% (38%)
Seriousness	29% (45%)	35% (2%)	19% (0%)	21% (45%)	23% (49%)
Multiple off.	16% (24%)	16% (2%)	1% (0%)	23% (38%)	7% (43%)
Attempt	1% (0%)	2% (0%)	0	0	3% (0%)
Intent	7% (36%)	10% (0%)	1% (0%)	4% (71%)	6% (27%)
Drugs	2% (17%)	2% (0%)	12% (0%)	1% (0%)	4% (57%)
Off. history	62% (76%)	67% (6%)	46% (1%)	84% (62%)	80% (36%)
Way of life	45% (55%)	0	0	0	0
Pers. circumst.	66% (67%)	18% (0%)	21% (3%)	43% (63%)	33% (39%)
Behaviour after	8% (62%)	4% (10%)	1% (0%)	0	1% (100%)
Cooperation	41% (29%)	9% (0%)	28% (0%)	61% (13%)	40% (24%)
Remorse	11% (25%)	26% (1%)	16% (0%)	56% (5%)	16% (10%)
Repar. damages	3% (82%)	2% (0%)	6% (0%)	7% (46%)	5% (56%)
General	0	0	0	0	0
Lack circumst.	10% (12%)	0	0	0	0
Time since	0% (0%)	7% (0%)	0	5% (44%)	7% (0%)
Future life	15% (12%)	0	0	1% (0%)	0
Cause of crime	5% (50%)	1% (33%)	1% (0%)	0	7% (46%)
Context	21% (63%)	0% (0%)	0	16% (61%)	0
Sanctions	19% (65%)	2% (0%)	0	1% (100%)	2% (67%)
Other	2% (67%)	2% (25%)	1% (0%)	2% (33%)	1% (50%)

Note: N: = 3,400 factors. The first number refers to the percentage of cases in which a factor was mentioned. The number in brackets means what percentage of these mentions were specified.

and Moldova, whose judges mention harm and seriousness much less commonly than offending history and cooperation.

The frequency with which courts consider individual factors likely reflects the difficulty of investigating certain factors. For example, defining the level of intent is inherently difficult, since no-one can directly read the offender's mind. Even though intent should influence a sentence in every case, it is rarely mentioned (at most 10% in Estonia). Similarly, courts rarely mentioned the reasons for committing the crime (cause of crime) as well. On the other hand, offending history or cooperation with authorities are well-documented factors and can thus be easily discussed and specified – and they are. Similarly, the non-specification level of some factors might reflect the difficulty of their operationalisation. For example, it is difficult to explain what constitutes true remorse. Not surprisingly, except in Czechia, courts specified it in at most 10% of decisions that mentioned remorse.

The second level of reasoning specifies the importance and direction of each factor. The results displayed in Figure 4.3 suggest that courts rarely

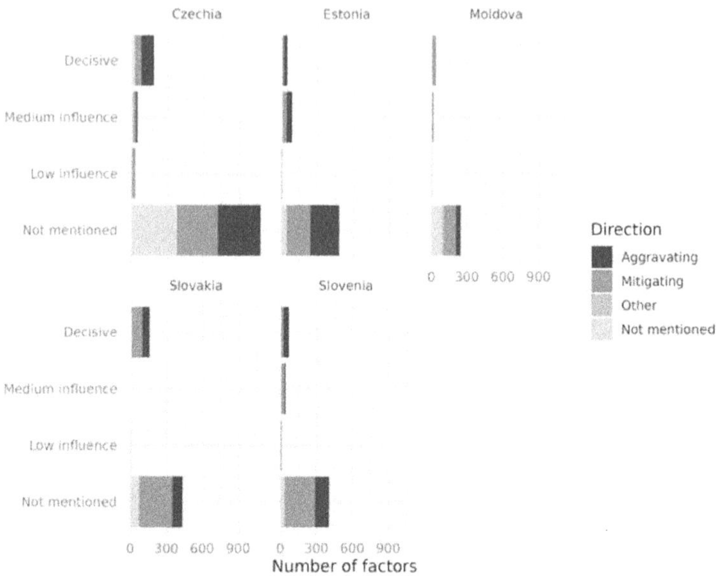

Figure 4.3 Factors' direction and importance by country

Note: N = 3,367 factors.

mention the factor's importance. If a court discusses a factor's importance, it assigns a decisive role to it. In such a case, the importance of a single factor court likely uses the factor to support a specific claim. An example might be an extensive criminal history supporting the decision to incarcerate. Medium and low influence of a factor was rarely invoked except for the case of Estonia, where factors with a medium role occurred more frequently. In Estonia, the different approach might result from an approach outlined by the Estonian Supreme Court, which started in the middle of a sentencing range and moved up or down depending upon the present factors; this requires judges to explicitly consider factors that do not even play a decisive role. Nevertheless, even in Estonia, factor importance was infrequently mentioned. Given the rare mentions of factor importance, we do not analyse it further. However, its low occurrence complicates the next step (weighing): weighing factors is only possible if their strength is at least approximately expressed.

Direction – whether a factor is aggravating or mitigating – is mentioned frequently, as shown in Figure 4.3. To consider it in more detail, we investigate the aggravating and mitigating roles of different factor categories in Figure 4.4. Offence-related factors are typically aggravating (with Estonia

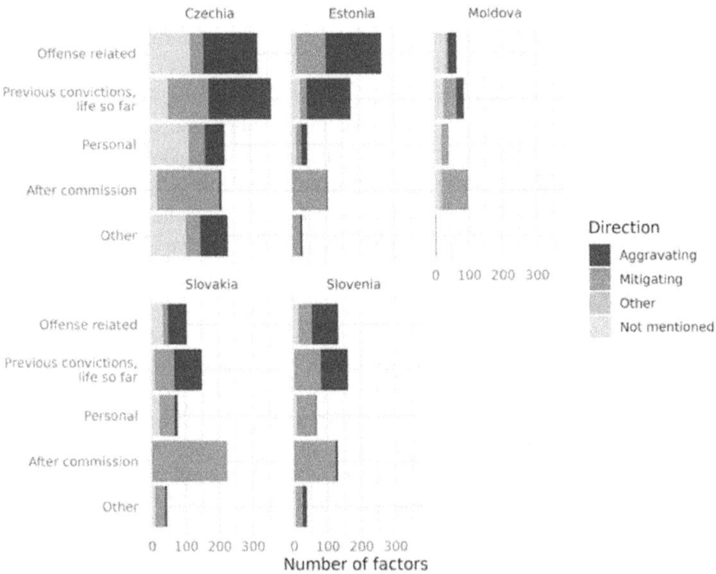

Figure 4.4 Direction of factors by categories and countries

Note: N = 3,396 factors.

and Slovenia considering them rather frequently as mitigating). This suggests that judges might compare committed offences primarily with those of low seriousness, with the result that offence-related factors play aggravating roles. The Estonian exception might reflect its specific approach in imposing sentences starting in the middle of a sentencing range, which inherently leads to offence-related factors more frequently playing a mitigating role.

Factors related to offenders' behaviour after commission almost always mitigate the sentence, which is unsurprising given that they mainly consist of guilty pleas. The largest category of factors – previous convictions and life so far – plays both mitigating and aggravating roles (except for the case of Estonia, where they only play aggravating roles). As studied criminal justice systems do not adhere to any specific theory of previous convictions, it seems that extensive criminal history likely aggravates, while none or limited criminal history typically mitigates. Previous convictions are likely not considered in a principled way, as an elaborated theory of previous convictions would likely lead to them being considered in a specific direction. For example, a progressive loss of mitigation approach (Frase & Roberts, 2019, pp. 31–33) would suggest that all previous convictions were mitigating.

Next, we investigate a connection between an imposed sentence, an offence category and a factor direction in Figure 4.5. Not surprisingly, previous convictions and life so far aggravate when judges impose non-suspended prison sentences, but mitigate (likely their non-existence mitigates) when imposing suspended prison sentences. When a court imposes a community sentence, it goes both ways. The mitigating role of personal circumstances when imposing suspended prison sentences can also be expected. Offence-related factors logically often aggravate when courts impose a non-suspended prison sentence, since the probability of incarceration increases with offence seriousness; they aggravate for other sentences as well, but less often.

The weighing of factors is the third level of reasoning required to understand each factor's role and how a final sentence was determined. Weighing happens sometimes, as shown in Figure 4.6, with a slight exception being Slovakia. It is also more commonly found when the primary imposed sentence is a non-suspended prison sentence, which is not surprising given the punitive bite of this sentence type and increased standards for reasoning following the imposition of a non-suspended prison sentence in some countries (although this is not true for the case of Moldova). Overall, however, weighing is relatively rare across the region.

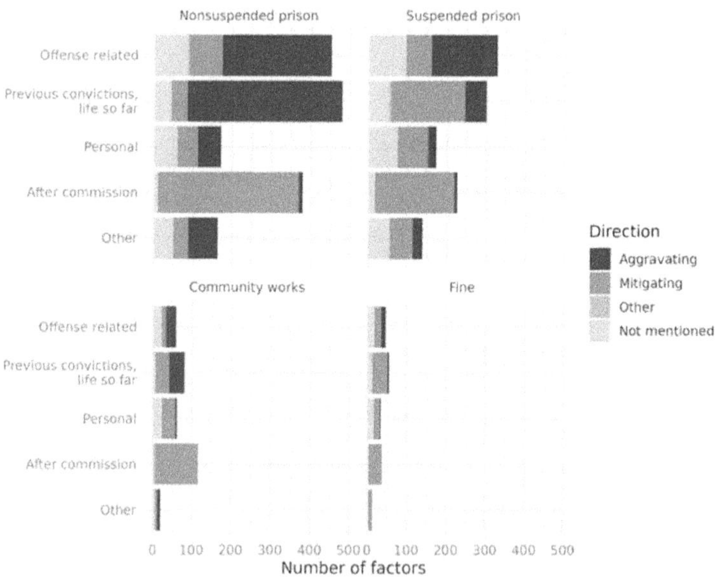

Figure 4.5 Importance of factors by type of sanction and factor type

Note: N = 3,330 factors.

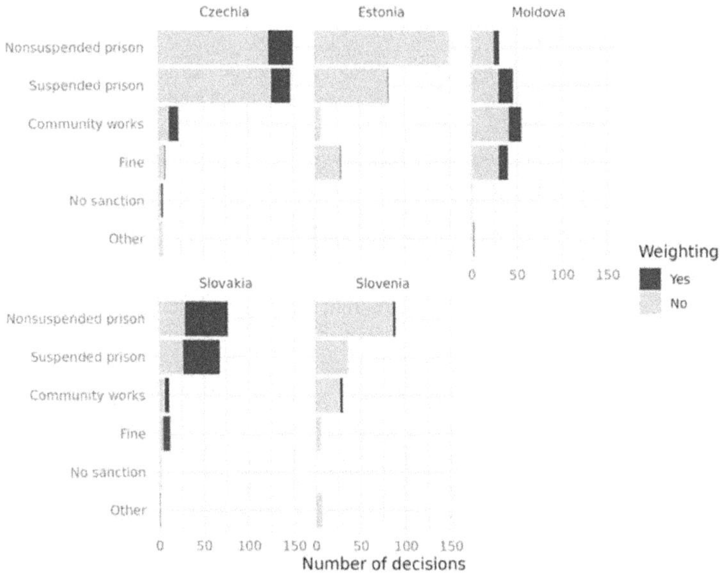

Figure 4.6 Weighing by country and sanction

Note: N = 1,121 decisions.

The three sentencing stages are largely unfulfilled across the region; the sentencing process thus cannot be reproduced by others based only (or primarily) on courts' written reasoning. Although judges and theorists across the region call for individualisation (Drápal & Plesničar, 2023), the mentioned factors are typically not specified, so what lies behind the general label of a factor is unclear. One can only speculate about the process of individualisation – if it has taken place – if one has access to a case file. Courts rarely mention the importance of factors even though they generally discuss their direction. This complicates the next step, weighing, which they seldom explain. The reader might thus glimpse potential thoughts and understand part of the judges' reasoning, but the imposition of a sentence remains a mystery.

Sentencing aims

For a long time, sentencing aims and judicial ideologies were emphasised as influencing sentencing (Hogarth, 1971). We thus investigate what sentencing aims judges express and whether the mention of a specific aim results in a discussion of factors associated with said aim. In other words, we investigate to what extent expressed sentencing aims are rhetoric and whether judges take them seriously.

We begin by discussing how often judges mention individual sentence aims in individual countries (Figure 4.7). Various consequentialist sentencing aims are emphasised several times more frequently than retribution, while retribution is never given as a country's most commonly mentioned sentencing aim. Regarding what consequentialist aims judges mention, Slovenian judges emphasise the role of specific deterrence while paying almost no attention to other sentencing aims. Estonian judges stress deterrence in both its specific and general forms but do not mention rehabilitation or incapacitation.[3] Czech judges try to influence offenders' behaviour for the future; they primarily emphasise rehabilitation but also want to deter offenders from further re-offending. Moldova and Slovakia emphasise several consequentialist sentencing aims, with Moldova not mentioning incapacitation. It almost seems that Moldovan judges use a formula which they repeat in every decision, as courts seem to mention the three consequentialist sentencing aims in most decisions. The extent to which differences between countries reflect different approaches of different countries we cannot say, as we have only studied what judges write, not what they do or think. Further research might test whether, for instance, Slovenian judges would prioritise the deterrent effect of sanctions, while Czech and Slovak judges would favour rehabilitation with a particular preference given to deterrence.

Mentioning a sentencing aim can be either a rhetorical or a genuine expression of why judges imposed a particular sentence. Courts would need to discuss whether certain factors count or do not count as a true expression. We focus on retribution, rehabilitation and incapacitation, as factors related to these sentencing aims can be easily identified. On the other hand, specific and general deterrence can be hardly linked to specific factors that judges would mention in their decisions.

Let us begin with retribution. If retribution is to guide judges, they should discuss (i) the offenders' intent, (ii) the seriousness of the behaviour, (iii) harm caused by the offender and, ideally, (iv) context. Courts rarely mentioned these factors when they emphasised retribution as the sentencing aim; they mentioned intent in 4.1% of cases, seriousness in 18.4%, harm in 15% and context in 7.7%, in which they emphasised retribution (although context was a write-in option). Thus, even though judges sometimes emphasise retribution as a guiding sentencing aim, associated factors which are necessary to impose a proportionate (deserved) sentence are typically not discussed.

If a judge mentions rehabilitation as the sentencing aim which guides sentence imposition, they should discuss at least two factors: why offender

3 This is likely due to the Penal Code (§ 56) which mentions retribution and specific and general deterrence among the factors that form the basis of the punishment, but omits rehabilitation and incapacitation. Still, retribution is typically not discussed.

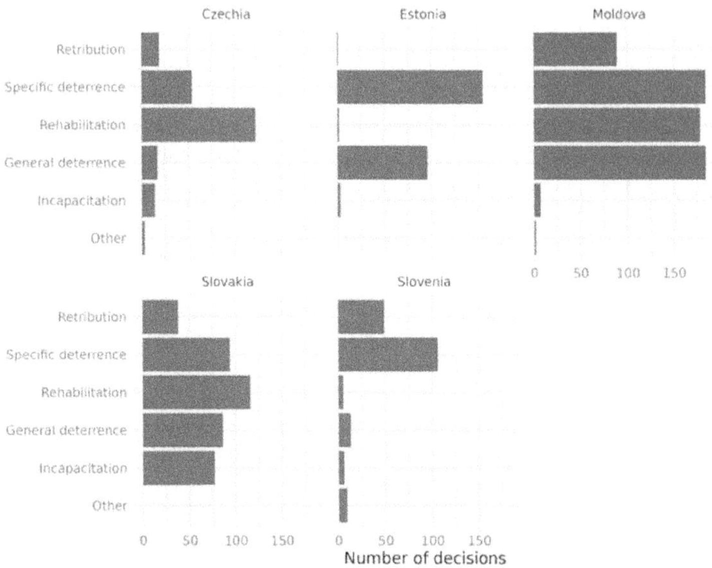

Figure 4.7 Sentencing aims by country

Note: N = 1,286.

committed the crime – so that an effective remedy can be taken to counter re-offending – and offenders' personal circumstances to help him/her desist from offending. However, when mentioning rehabilitation as a sentencing aim, judges only discussed the causes of crimes in 1.2% of decisions, and personal circumstances were mentioned in 33.5%. Again, the language of rehabilitation seems to be a rhetorical exercise not backed up by a discussion of relevant factors.

When courts mention incapacitation among sentencing aims, they should discuss re-offending risk. Since none of the studied countries provide judges with re-offending predictions, judges must assess it themselves. The factor which judges should primarily examine to determine whether to incapacitate an offender is previous convictions, a factor used most often in various re-offending prediction algorithms (Monahan & Skeem, 2016). When judges mention incapacitation as a sentencing aim, they discuss it in 78.5% of cases.

Overall, expressions of sentencing aims are mostly about rhetoric that is not followed up by a discussion of factors that would have to be considered to fulfil these aims. We should thus regard expressions of sentencing aims at least with a strong dose of scepticism. Nevertheless, since we do not know what influenced the imposed sentences in the studied cases, we should be cautious about discarding them altogether. However, given the judges' reluctance to follow a mention of a sentencing aim with specific factors associated with it, we should certainly not take mentions of sentencing aims at face value. The most likely interpretation of the mentions of sentencing aims would be to treat them as performative acts that are addressed to different audiences and through which judges can re-assure themselves of doing justice, bridging the gap between ideal and everyday practice (Tata, 2019). For post-communist judges, justice seems to be reflected primarily in consequentialist (utilitarian) sentencing aims, echoing communist rhetoric.

Reasoning as storytelling

Finally, we investigate how frequently judges present reasoning as a story, as discussed in Chapter 3 and as theorised by Tata (1997, 2020, pp. 64–65), who suggests that – especially in cases of multiple offending – judges construct whole-case stories. Our results do not suggest that post-communist judges present their reasoning as a story; this occurred only in 1.7% of cases.

Judges might not construct reasoning as a story, but they may do so unintentionally by discussing all the relevant features of a story. We thus studied the frequency of five questions describing a story ("what," "who," "how," "context" and "what effect"); our results are displayed in Figure 4.8. In all countries – except for Estonia – the person of the offender ("who did it?") is the central question to which judges provide answers. What and how it happened are secondary points, and the context and effect are rare. This amplifies

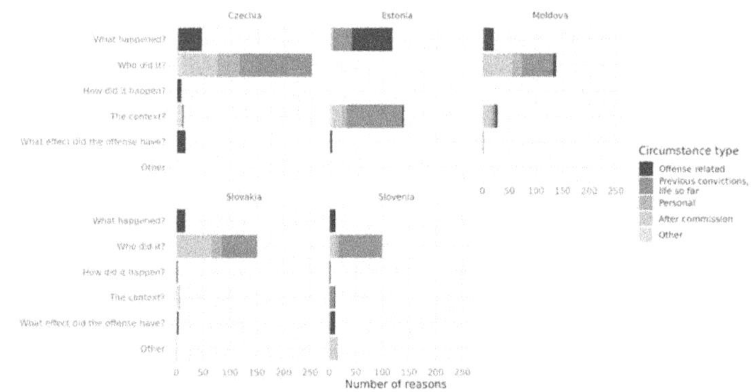

Figure 4.8 Five questions by factor type and country

Note: N = 1,108. We excluded decisions which did not mention at least one factor.

the message already communicated by the sentencing aims: the person of the offender (and, hence, the emphasis placed on the consequentialist aims) is more important than the offence (in which the emphasis is placed on the retributivist aim).

Estonia seems to differ, yet it is the result of a different classification of "context"; previous convictions were considered within "context" and not within "who". Even with this correction, Estonia would remain different, with a more significant emphasis on "what", likely due to the fact that Estonian Penal code mentions the offender's guilt as the primary basis for a punishment (§ 56). Otherwise, the classification seems to be representative, as offence-related factors are linked with questions "what", "how", and "what effect," and previous convictions, life so far, personal factors and behaviour after commission are primarily linked to "who" and "context."

Discussion

Reasons provided for imposed sentences are the only manifestation of how post-communist judges use the broad discretion they are provided. Judges, however, do not take stock of this opportunity – the general level of reasoning is deficient. Judges mention a small number of factors, and most of them are not specified. Explanation of the importance of individual factors and their weighing is rare or non-existent. Thus, no-one can fully understand why a specific sentence was imposed, and it is difficult to ascertain even a partial understanding of the reasons behind sentence imposition. Several years ago, a high-ranking judge explained this to one of the authors when discussing the quality of reason-giving: one needs to know the case file to understand why a sentence was imposed; simply reading the reasoned verdict is not enough. Given the broad discretion offered in weighing factors, we are not confident that a case file would resolve it (although we grant that it will likely help at least a little). The low level of accountability might be problematic for the sentencing system in the long run; if judges are unwilling to explain their use of broad entrusted discretion, politicians might limit it.

Given the importance of the individualisation principle in the region, one is left to wonder whether individualisation might be only a rhetorical or wishful declaration of what could be; presently, individualisation means that judges cannot be held accountable for their decisions. The most frequently mentioned factors suggest that judges likely individualise the sentence to the offender and the behaviour after the offence. Previous convictions, personal circumstances and behaviour after commission dominate sentence justifications, with courts mentioning offence-related factors less frequently. Individualisation, as carried out in post-communist countries, means fitting the case to an offender, not to an offence.

Focus on the offender and not on the offence is further emphasised by the sentencing aims that judges mention. Consequentialist goals dominate here.

Judges sometimes mention a retributivist (proportionalist) perspective, but not very frequently. The same story is told by answers provided by judges; they predominantly relate to who committed the offence but do not focus on what and how it was committed. Sentencing is thus offender-centred, not offence-centred (with Estonia being the most tilted towards offence-centred), complicating possible proportionality-based reforms akin to those found in Nordic countries.

If only courts really tailored the decision to the offender. Even though judges emphasised consequentialist goals when we investigated whether judges mentioned factors associated with the sentencing aims they mentioned, they did it only to a limited extent. When emphasising rehabilitation, judges rarely discussed the causes of crime and personal circumstances, while, when emphasising incapacitation, judges in most cases mentioned previous convictions. The insufficient link between sentencing aims and the discussed factors appears when retribution is also mentioned; offender's intent, offence seriousness, harm and context were typically not discussed. Sentencing aims thus likely serve as a rhetorical, but not an actual, explanation of why judges impose a sentence.

Even though judges present sentencing as offender-centred, they do not actually study and react to the causes of crime and offenders' personal circumstances. Inconsistency between the expression of sentencing aims and the discussion of associated factors suggests a paradigm shift which could be difficult to operationalise. If post-communist countries decide to follow, for example, Nordic countries in emphasising proportionality, two reforms would be necessary. First, the sentencing aim paradigm would need to change; the system would need to accept that attention needs to be paid to an offence at least as much as to an offender (as in many respects is found in Estonia). Secondly, judges would need to acknowledge that a paradigm shift should result in judges changing their approach to sentencing. The rhetorical use of sentencing aims when it is not followed by consideration of relevant factors results in a possible reform being less likely realisable than if no sentencing aims were mentioned or if judges were accustomed to their practice following rhetoric.

The low quality of reasoning is not surprising, given the broad discretion and the little guidance provided to judges. If judges are not instructed on the role of individual principles depending upon their specifications, can we really expect judges to provide detailed reasoning? It would be difficult for them, as in systems without sufficient guidance, their decision is – at least to some extent – intuitive. Providing detailed written reasons would require them to develop a thought process that likely did not occur when they arrived at a specific sentence. This is a paradox of over-emphasised individualisation; the broad discretion given requires judges to be accountable for its use, yet the vagueness of rules and little guidance provided to judges make it (very) difficult for them to provide understandable reasoning.

The lack of instruction and suggestions on proper reasoning further contributes to the low quality of reason-giving. There were no detailed discussions concerning how reasoning should look in the examined countries. The three-stage model described in Chapter 3 has not been mentioned in post-communist countries prior to our study (unsurprisingly, however, as it has been published only in Dutch so far). Judges were thus expected to devise an appropriate way to justify imposed sentences on their own, making principled reason-giving even more challenging to achieve.

The quality of reason-giving provided by first-level courts further complicates the role of other actors within the criminal justice system, especially appellate and supreme courts. If specific principles are not elaborated in detail by first-level courts, appellate and supreme courts have to guess why lower courts made a decision, resulting in difficulties in deciding on the role of a specific factor in a particular setting. We discuss the role of appellate courts and the reactions of appellate courts to this situation in Chapter 5. Poor quality of the justification also complicates the work of researchers or journalists who cannot use a written verdict to understand why a specific sentence was imposed.

A possible solution would be to specify the sentencing process and the reason-giving design at the same time. This would help judges arrive at what sentences to impose and enable others to understand why a specific sentence was imposed. In Chapter 7, we thus propose a solution to this problem by structuring the decision-making process; the proposed idea might also be easily used as a template for a principled sentence reasoning.

Finally, when thinking about how to improve the current situation, we discuss the exceptions to providing written reasoning for sentences, due to which reason-giving is typically an exception, although it is officially a rule. Specifically, we discuss the appropriateness of not providing reasoning (i) when the judge decides by a penal order, (ii) following a plea agreement, and (iii) when a simplified verdict is issued.

A penal order is the easiest way for a judge to conclude a case: describe the behaviour, set a sentence, send a letter, and see whether the offender objects to the decision. A penal order does not need to include reasoning relating to guilt, as the defendant is well aware of whether the described behaviour reflects his or her true behaviour and can file an objection against it. A sentence is different; a defendant cannot ascertain whether the imposed sentence is just or not and whether the court based it on factors which reflect reality or not. The defendant thus needs to understand why a sentence was imposed to consider objecting against it being based on false information or improper considerations. Penal orders thus might include sentence justifications, which should not be time-consuming as judges should already know why they imposed a specific sentence. An exception might be in systems that must operate very efficiently and allow only lenient sentences via a penal order (e.g., when it is impossible to incarcerate the offender). Time pressures in such settings could vindicate judges from not providing reasons, as the penal order could be construed as an informal plea-bargaining suggestion.

Plea agreements are different because the reasons communicate the sentence justification primarily to the public, but not to the offender. While the difference is important, the nature of plea bargaining – discounts and bargaining, instead of impartial justice – might require written reasons to be given, especially when imposing sentences for serious offences. Detailed justification could persuade the public that the court imposed a just sentence, not distorted by improper secret dealings, enabling the rich and powerful to escape just punishment.

The last exception to providing written reasoning relates to simplified verdicts. The appropriateness of providing written justifications only when parties file an appeal or waive their right to an appeal depends upon the quality of oral reasoning. If oral reasoning is sufficiently detailed, written reasoning would not be necessary. However, it is unreasonable to expect oral reasoning to be of higher quality than the written one analysed in this chapter. Based on oral reasoning, parties likely cannot understand why a court imposed a certain sentence, complicating the activity of appealing against wrong specification and consideration of the factors. We are not sure to what extent one can expect oral reasoning to be improved without requiring the provision of written reasoning. Detailed reasoning prepared before the announcement of the sentence would help judges to provide proper oral reasoning and help parties consider whether to file an appeal. Given that the preparation of detailed reasoning for oral presentation is very close to providing a written one, requiring written reasons should not be time-consuming for judges.

Overall, we believe that the exceptions to the general rule about providing reasons for sentences should be reconsidered. We need to separate the duty to justify decisions on guilt and sentence, bringing the continental systems closer to the two-stage common-law approach. Given that judges have thoroughly considered why they impose certain sentences, explaining them in a structured form (in which the structure would be pre-defined, not the phrases that should be used) should not be time-consuming. Instead, the structured form should help judges to arrive at a proper sentence, and, as they will have provided their reasoning clearly, we find it likely that parties would not appeal. Structuring reason-giving would thus be beneficial for the judges, the parties and the public.

5 Justifying sentence changes at appellate courts

Jakub Drápal and Tomáš Vanča

Introduction

The principle of the rule of law necessitates the ability to review any public authority's limitation of human rights; such decisions cannot be unchecked. Given that criminal sentences are the most intrusive measure which a state can employ against an individual, the European Convention on Human Rights unsurprisingly foresees a right to review the sentence by appellate courts.[1] These typically represent the only instance that can prevent first-level courts from abusing the often broad discretion provided in sentencing. Additionally, appellate courts are ideally placed to provide first-level courts with the necessary feedback regarding how they employ discretion. Sentence appellate review is thus important both in relation to a specific case – so that a fair and consistent sentence is imposed – and in explaining sentencing principles which contribute to consistent sentencing in general (Labbe, 1977; Marshall, 2011; O'Malley, 2011, p. 114; Thomas, 2003). The fulfilment of these aims is, however, not as easy as one might expect.

The role of appellate courts is largely limited by (i) the quality of reasoning from first-level courts and (ii) the extent to which appellate courts are willing to correct sentences imposed by first-level courts. The first of these two issues relates to how appellate courts review sentences (*the method of review*): do they review the process which the first-level court has taken, or do they review the outcome? Moreover, does their choice depend on how well the first-level courts justify their sentences? The second issue relates to what mistakes appellate courts (should) correct (*the standard of review*). Both the chosen method and the standard of review reveal to what extent appellate courts in individual countries might correct imposed sentences and whether appellate courts might guide first-level courts in establishing better-structuring discretion.

In this chapter, we first discuss different views on the method and standard of review and then consider how choices between different options impact the

1 Protocol no. 7, article 2, sec. 1.

DOI: 10.4324/9781003470670-5

appellate courts' dual responsibility: to impose fair sentences and to develop and uphold sentencing jurisprudence. We do this without linking this debate to any specific sentencing system. We then study the justification of Czech appellate courts to change a sentence by showing how these issues are connected with well-functioning appellate courts. We begin by providing a short introduction to the context and presenting the sample and methods. Then we discuss the results in which we focus on what decisions appellate courts made, how they justified them and to what extent these decisions outline sentencing principles for future decision-making. We conclude the case study by discussing why appellate review in the Czech Republic cannot provide the requested results, and we close the chapter by outlining principles for a well-functioning sentence appellate review within a limited retributivist framework.[2]

Method of review

There is no single "gold standard" or "best answer" sentence. Consequently, sentencing theorists argue that a principled process (manifesting a consistency of approach) is more important than the outcome, and that a principled and consistent outcome should result from a principled and consistent approach (Harris, 2022, pp. 25–38). As for what this means for sentence appellate review, an appellate court should primarily revise the process[3] rather than the outcome. Ideally, the individual steps taken by first-level courts should be re-traced, and appellate courts should evaluate whether these steps were correctly executed: were all factors considered correctly specified, given the appropriate importance and properly weighted (see Chapter 3)? Arguably, these considerations are more important than what outcome was reached – as there is no other way how to judge whether the outcome was correct or not.

Such an approach has several important advantages. Firstly, the review of individual decisions made at different points in time should reveal different types of mistakes that simple re-sentencing by appellate courts might miss. Secondly, it helps everyone to understand what was done incorrectly, and provide guidance on future decision-making for first-level courts. As a result, more detailed specification of sentencing principles and an ensuing "sentencing jurisprudence" could arise. The quality of such jurisprudence would necessarily be linked to a chosen standard of review: when the less important

2 This chapter is based on a Czech article which discusses in detail practices of Czech appellate courts (Vanča & Drápal, 2023). The translation of parts of this article was carried out when this chapter was written.

3 When employing the term "sentencing process," we mean how a sentence was formulated in a particular case, the explanation of what factors were involved and in what way they were considered. In contrast to this, "sentencing procedure" encompasses various procedural steps taken when a sentence is imposed, including sentence recommendations, imposition of sentences by first-level courts and imposition of sentences by appellate courts.

mistakes have been corrected, the more detailed sentencing jurisprudence would appear. Finally, appellate courts would be required to provide precise reasons for interfering with the decision of the first-level court. Who guards the guardians? There is little oversight over appellate courts; requiring them to justify what factors they have considered differently than the first-level courts and why would limit the arbitrariness of the appellate courts' decisions, increasing their accountability and advancing principled sentencing in general.

Reviewing the sentencing process is ideal but, unfortunately, unimaginable in most countries. This is because any review of the process requires a clearly defined sentencing process and its application in practice; first-level courts would have to justify sentences in detail and in a structured way. Both requirements are, however, unfulfilled in most systems. In Chapter 7, we outline how a sentencing process (protocol) could be structured, yet such (or any kind of) structuring is rare across the world. First-level courts are not provided with any guidance regarding how they should structure sentencing process and their decisions. Not surprisingly, as we show in Chapter 4, the level of reasoning is low. As a result, appellate courts do not have the opportunity to review the sentencing process of first-level courts. They would first have to compel first-level courts to follow certain protocols, and only then could they review it. It is, however, hardly imaginable for them to start doing it by themselves, as this would entail a complete policy change coupled with interfering with almost every decision made by first-level courts.

Appellate courts are thus left with the option of reviewing only the outcome – the imposed sentence – and not the process (which is sometimes labelled "re-sentencing" at the appellate level (Rosenbaum, 2013)).[4] They, therefore, have to determine what sentence they would impose themselves and then compare this sentence with the sentence imposed by the first-instance court. If the discrepancy is substantial according to the standard of review, the appellate court imposes a new sentence. The level of difficulty in conducting such a review depends upon how appellate courts approach it; they might either reconstruct the sentencing process – which would be rather difficult, as it might require additional evidence being presented – or they might make an educated guess (an instinctive synthesis), which is likely an easier option and thus probably also the more frequently taken path. However, without detailed explanations of why they made a certain decision, appellate courts might be viewed mainly as courts "with a bigger stamp," ones whose decisions are accepted due to their hierarchical position rather than because of their convincing nature.

4 Similarly, appellate courts can review only the outcome when they review decisions for which no reasoning is provided.

In such situations, appellate courts cannot be expected to explain in detail why they interfered (or did not interfere) with first-level courts' decisions. No or limited indication regarding what mistakes were made and why certain factors were given an inappropriate role means that it will be difficult or impossible to develop sentencing principles in general. Consequently, although the development of jurisprudence is one of the essential elements of layered decision-making (Freiberg & Sallmann, 2008), this can hardly happen if only an outcome – and not the process and arguments supporting the initial decision – is reviewed. The lack of structured decision-making thus disables the proper fulfilment of basic functions of an appellate review. We need to be aware of the dilemma that, even though in theory an appellate review could be a very useful tool, the context within which it operates might significantly reduce its effectiveness.

Standard of review

Whatever method of review is chosen, the statutory provisions need to specify the level of incorrectness of sentences required for appellate courts to change them. There are various degrees of incorrectness on an imaginable scale, ranging from a merely incorrect sentence to an unreasonable one and even to a grossly disproportionate sentence. To simplify the discussion, we outline two different approaches: (i) preventing excesses and (ii) correcting even mildly improper decisions.

The prevention of excesses – as is reflected by terms like "unreasonableness," "wrong in principle," "abuse of discretion" or "gross disproportionality" – is the typical standard of review for several reasons. From a pragmatic viewpoint, the correction of large numbers of decisions would be impractical as it would be very time-consuming. If appellate courts change the sentence, even if the difference would be minimal, large numbers of defendants would file appeals. This would be especially true in systems in which, if only a defendant appeals, an appellate court cannot aggravate the sentence (which, in Europe, is the dominating paradigm); in such systems, defendants have nothing to lose and can only gain. Correcting even mildly improper decisions would thus require many appellate judges, which would be a significant financial burden and thus unlikely to happen.

The lack of sentencing principles in almost all countries further complicates the correction of minor missteps. Requiring appellate courts to make a principled distinction between, for example, similar but slightly different versions of criminal history requires support from academia to be able to explain the roles of individual sentencing principles on an at least semi-general level. Such support is, however, typically lacking. Appellate courts would thus have to decide on sentencing principles in detail without any theoretical foundations, which will likely not result in a principled and complex approach. In this scenario, appellate courts would decide issues on a case-by-case basis without having any framework within which to embed the individual principles. If a system wants to go beyond correcting blatant excesses such that appellate courts can contribute to a principled sentencing being formed, appellate courts first need to be supported by academics in their endeavours.

Lastly, appellate courts might be reluctant to correct even mildly improper decisions, as the core evidence is presented in front of first-level courts; in continental systems, first-level judges observe the offender throughout the entire trial, influencing their decision. On the other hand, appellate courts typically review the sentence based on written evidence (Marshall, 2011). Appellate courts are thus expected to provide certain leeway for – and so to defer to – first-level courts (Freiberg & Sallmann, 2008). Given there is no "gold standard" sentence, correcting even minor details of sentences might thus go against the judicial approach to sentencing and possibly even against missing important details.[5]

Should, then, appellate courts change only excessive sentences? This seems to be the reasonable (and typically the only possible) option, although the definition of "excessive" can vary. Correcting only excessive sentences will, however, result in that – and typically in nothing else. Therefore, if only excesses are corrected, we should not expect an appellate review to produce detailed sentencing jurisprudence.

For a principled sentencing jurisprudence to occur within a framework which corrects only excessive sentences, appellate courts would have to routinely mention that first-level courts did not decide correctly and explain why, while not overturning the decision in the case that the extent of the mistake does not fulfil the standard of review. We do not believe that appellate courts would be willing to do this, as it would undermine confidence in the judiciary. Defendants and the public would regularly hear that first-level courts did not do their job properly, but that the system is unwilling to do anything about it. We do not think that the judiciary wishes to take this approach; the creation of a principled sentencing jurisprudence is likely something the judiciary would be willing to sacrifice in order for the legitimacy of the judicial system to be preserved.

Disclosing principled reasoning only when correcting excesses thus cannot lead to a detailed principled sentencing jurisprudence, as there would be no recommendations regarding inappropriate or incorrect decisions that were not excessive. The unifying role of the appellate courts would be relatively small, since the appellate courts would comment only on excesses, but the first-instance courts would not know when they decided "only" in an inappropriate fashion. This criticism was succinctly expressed by Hessick: "The approval of one district court's policy as reasonable does not mean that other

5 On the other hand, personal experience with the offender might play too large a role.

district courts, or even the same district court, must apply that same policy in the future to similar cases" (Hessick, 2009, p. 743).

A case study: Czech appellate courts

To provide insights into how appellate courts decide in practice, we have analysed decisions by which Czech appellate courts change a sentence imposed by a first-level court. In studying the reasons given for their decisions, we have focused on the method and standard of review and the way in which appellate courts communicate their findings to first-level courts. Initially, we provide a context to our discussion by presenting the basic features of the Czech appellate procedure and noting the frequency of appeals. After a brief discussion of the employed method and the analysed sample, we present how appellate courts change sentences imposed by first-level courts (the standard of review), how they justify the changes (the method of a review) and the way they communicate them, considering in what scope appellate courts address the first-level courts' argumentation and provide general recommendations for future decision-making. We close by reflecting on what the findings tell us about the functioning of appellate courts in a system that offers judges broad discretion.

Especially for readers from common-law countries, we find it important to emphasise that the appellate review of sentences has a very long tradition in continental legal systems, much longer than the one in common-law systems. The possibility to review sentences on appeals appeared in English common law in 1907 and, even though in the United States some states introduced it a few decades earlier (Mueller, 1961; Rosenbaum, 2013), "for the greater part of American history, appellate review of federal criminal sentences was nonexistent in most cases" (Hessick & Hessick, 2008, p. 5). In contrast, sentence appeals on the mainland of the European continent were part of the criminal procedure before the United States was founded. Moreover, these appeals likely function better since continental systems rely more on written evidence (Marshall, 2011). Czechia is in this respect no different; a broadly conceived right to appeal against an imposed sentence has existed at least since the middle of the 19th century.

Context: Czech appellate procedure and its frequency

An appeal against a sentence can be filed against any first-level court judgment in the Czech Republic, either by a prosecution or a defendant. If an appeal is filed solely in favour of the defendant, the appellate court cannot change the first-level court's judgment to the detriment of the defendant. Appellate courts are expected to quash the decision if the sentence is disproportionate[6]

6 Section 258/1/e of the Code of Criminal Procedure.

and impose a new sentence if they can do so based on available evidence (typically, appellate courts decide on their own and do not return the case to a first-level court for a new hearing). The vague concept of "disproportionate" punishment has been defined by appellate courts as requiring a significant difference between the imposed sentence and the one deemed correct by the appellate court (Vanča & Drápal, 2023). The standard of review is therefore aimed at correcting excesses rather than at imposing correct or appropriate punishments, but no one knows whether this standard is upheld in practice.

Appeals are a relatively frequent phenomenon in the Czech criminal procedure; an appeal is filed by either a defendant or a prosecutor in approximately every tenth case. Using official administrative data from 2007 to 2022, we analysed the frequency of appeals against two types of courts: district courts (N = 931,182 decisions) and regional courts (N = 14,864 decisions). The vast majority of these cases were dealt with by 86 district courts, except for the most serious ones, which were dealt with by 8 regional courts. Regional courts also serve as appellate courts when an appeal is filed against a district court decision. Appeals against first-level decisions of regional courts are resolved by two high courts. The Supreme Court does not in general decide on sentencing.

Appeals have been filed against 11.4% of district courts decisions, with one-quarter being changed on an appeal. Two-thirds of the changed decisions result in only a sentence change, while one third results in a different decision on guilt (and possibly also on a sentence).[7] Appeals are overwhelmingly filed by defendants, but when an appeal is filed by the prosecutor, he or she has a substantially higher chance of success. Appeals against the decisions of regional courts are much more frequent, being filed against 75.5% of decisions, and these decisions are frequently changed on appeal. Specifically, two out of five appeals were successful, while only the sentence was changed in slightly more than half of the cases. The decision on guilt (and possibly sentence as well) was changed in less than half of the cases.[8]

These statistics illustrate that compared with common-law countries, appeals are more common and appellate courts regularly rule on sentences. For example, U.S. federal courts reversed only 44 sentences for substantive unreasonableness over a period of 6 years (Rosenbaum, 2013). In England and Wales, appeals were heard by Crown courts against 0.5% of defendants sentenced at magistrate courts and 2%–2.7% of defendants sentenced in Crown courts. These allowed appeals represented approximately half of the appeals made against magistrate courts and one-quarter of cases filed against

7 The data does not contain information on whether the appeal was filed against a guilt or a sentence. However, even if filed against a guilt, the appellate court can typically review only the sentence.

8 We elaborate on these statistics elsewhere (Vanča & Drápal, 2023).

Crown court decisions (Jacobson, 2013). This suggests that Czech appellate courts may have even more opportunities to formulate sentencing jurisprudence – as they process more cases on appeal – than common-law systems.

Sample and method

We analysed appeals filed against decisions of first-level district courts, as these courts deal with the vast majority of decisions, and the role of appellate courts is therefore the most important. We started with all criminal decisions that acquired legal force in 2016 (N = 77,621), further limiting them to district court cases in which a sentence was imposed, in which no aggregate or conjoint sentence was imposed and in which the defendant was not a juvenile (N = 57,729). Appeal was filed against 12.1% of such decisions, with 1.5% of cases resulting in a more lenient sentence following an appeal (without any change with regard to guilt) and 0.7% of cases resulting in a more serious sentence following an appeal. We randomly selected 151 decisions from both of these groups using a random sampling method stratified at the level of appellate courts. We have, therefore, focused on decisions which change the sentence, and we can say little or nothing about decisions that do not change the sentence.[9]

We obtained the decisions of district (first-level) and appellate courts in cooperation with regional courts and through a Freedom of Information request; eight cases were excluded from the sample due to over-anonymisation or because the decisions were not provided. We employed content analysis to examine how appellate courts justified the sentence change. We sought answers to three basic questions linked to how appellate courts change sentences: how they change the punishment, on what basis, and the extent to which they try to draw general conclusions from their decisions. One shortcoming of our approach is that the content analysis was performed by only one person who also participated in defining the recorded variables. This can increase the uncertainty of the results, especially regarding more subjective categories (i.e., not the types of punishments imposed but whether there was a weighing of circumstances).[10]

We recorded information about the decisions made by first-level and appellate courts, the justifications provided by appellate courts with regard to what sentences appellate court imposed and the communication of the

9 Nevertheless, it would be interesting to examine, for example, whether appellate courts admitted that the sentence was not appropriate but was not sufficiently disproportionate to warrant a change.

10 The control of the procedure of coding the punishments was carried out by checking a random sample of a part of the coded decisions and comparing them with the data recorded in the criminal statistics sheets.

reasons and guidance towards first-level courts. In rccording the reasons that led appellate courts to change a sentence, we recorded various factors related to the offender's behaviour after the crime, the nature and seriousness of the criminal activity, personal circumstances and current lifestyle (as discussed in Chapter 4). In order for a factor to be recorded, it had to be evaluated by the appellate court; it was not enough if it was simply mentioned in the introductory part of the decision. We also studied if courts fulfil the three stages of reasoning (see Chapter 3): specification, importance and weighing. Finally, we documented whether appellate courts attempted to draw general conclusions by formulating rules and what those rules were. An appellate court either had to explicitly mention that courts should proceed in future similarly for us to classify it as a rule or the rule had to be largely generalised.

Types of changes: standard of review

Analysing the standard of review is not an easy task as appellate courts can change the primary sanction type, the amount of the primary sanction or the types and amounts of secondary sanctions – or make a combination of these changes. The change might be marginal, such as a forfeiture of insubstantial things, or fundamental, such as a suspension of a 3-year prison sentence. To identify the standard of review as applied by appellate courts, we need to create a ranking of sentence changes from the most serious to the less serious ones and record how often appellate courts made these changes. We chose to record the most important change and not the less important ones, as it would have otherwise been virtually impossible to present the results.

In Table 5.1, we show what changes appellate courts made. At least half of the changes without doubt fulfil the criteria set by the code of criminal procedure (sentence imposed by a first-level court being disproportionate): whether a suspended or a non-suspended prison sentence should be imposed and if a non-suspended prison sentence was increased or decreased by at least 25%. Other changes – except important changes to a suspended prison sentence's length – do not seem to primarily relate to proportionality, but mainly deal with the appropriateness (or reasonableness) of sanctions. This suggests that Czech appellate courts go beyond the standard of review prescribed by the code of criminal procedure.[11] Our findings are in line with concerns about appellate courts from other jurisdictions about their "tinkering" (Freiberg & Sallmann, 2008) and "wild inconsistency" (Rosenbaum, 2013) in choosing when to interfere.

This approach of appellate courts is, however, understandable; if they are the only ones able to correct the sentence, appellate courts are likely willing to

11 Additional analysis relating e.g., to changes in length of individual sanctions are described in detail elsewhere (Vanča & Drápal, 2023).

Table 5.1 Sentence changes resulting from an appeal

Difference due to decision by appellate courts	*N*	*Percentage*	*Cumulative percentage*
(Non-)imposition of a non-suspended prison sentence	95	32.5	32.5
The length of a non-suspended prison sentence was increased/decreased by at least 50% compared with the original sentence	34	11.6	44.1
The length of a non-suspended prison sentence was increased/decreased by 25%–50% compared with the original sentence	29	9.9	54
The length of a non-suspended prison sentence was increased/decreased by less than 25% compared with the original sentence	12	4.1	58.1
A different primary sanction was imposed	22	7.5	65.6
A secondary sanction was added/removed	23	7.9	73.5
Length of a suspended prison sentence was increased/decreased by at least 50% compared with the original sentence	25	8.6	82.1
Length of a suspended prison sentence was increased/decreased by less than 50% compared with the original sentence	9	3.1	85.2
Length of other primary sanctions was changed	19	6.5	91.7
Type of prison where the sentence is served was changed	5	1.7	93.4
Other change	19	6.5	99.9

Note: If the case falls within a higher category, it is no longer counted in a lower one.

interfere even if it is not necessary from the viewpoint of proportionality. This highlights the need to further elaborate the standard of review; proportionality is clearly not sufficient, yet no one knows what the proper standard of review should be as appellate courts operate beyond possibilities provided by the law and jurisprudence. This uncertainty might contribute to a higher number of appeals motivated by the defendants' "what if" attitude.

Method of the review

We next focused on how appellate courts reviewed first-level courts' decisions. It is impossible to follow a court's decision-making directly, so we derived the method of review from decisions. First, we considered how many factors appellate courts mentioned (Czech law foresees 70 possible factors to influence sentencing; see Chapter 7). Appellate courts mentioned on average 2.5 factors per case. We interpret this to mean that appellate courts very likely did not analyse all the factors again, but only focused on those which – for some unknown reason – led them to intervene. This, however, does not mean that appellate courts reviewed the process and only mentioned factors which were incorrectly specified. First-level courts' justifications are of low quality and do not enable a simple correction of two or three factors (see Chapter 4). Instead, appellate courts intuitively selected a few factors that, in their opinion, stood in stark contrast with the imposed sentence.

The only method of review which appellate courts can take is to determine what sentence should be imposed and compare the outcomes. In determining the sentence, the low number of mentioned factors suggests that appellate courts strike down first-level courts intuitively and justify it by emphasising the few factors that first-level courts – according to appellate courts – did not properly consider. Regarding the three steps outlined in Chapter 3, the circumstances were specified (with respect to the offender) in 86.4% of factors, a figure which outperformed first-level courts (see Chapter 4). This is a positive sign regarding the creation of a sentencing jurisprudence, as specification is the key to distinguish nuances in the application of principles.[12] The importance of a factor (the direction and an approximate weight) was discussed for 52.6% of factors. Finally, appellate courts indicated how they weighed factors in only 36% of cases, which is problematic. As a result, in the majority of cases, to ascertain why a certain decision was made was unclear in both first-level and appellate courts' cases; first-level courts intuitively imposed a sentence (and provided few reasons for it) and appellate courts intuitively corrected the sentence (and mentioned few reasons why).[13]

We then examined what factors appellate courts mentioned most frequently. The code of criminal procedure foresaw proportionality as the guiding principle, leading us to expect that offence-related characteristics would primarily influence why appellate courts change first-level courts' decisions. However, this was not the case. In Table 5.2, we list ten factors that appellate courts mentioned most frequently in the argumentative part of the verdict (but not when recapitulating the case). These results reveal that offender-related factors dominated the appellate courts' decisions. Different versions of criminal history, confession, cooperation and regret were the most commonly mentioned factors; among the ten most mentioned factors, only two factors directly related to the offence, both representing certain forms of multiple offending. This corroborates the findings from Chapter 4, which suggest that Czech courts focus more on an offender than on an offence.

12 However, a different person coded first-level courts' decisions employed in Chapter 4 and appellate courts' decisions; the differences might be partly due to the subjective perspective on what constituted specification.

13 It is possible that first-level and appellate courts internally assessed all factors and simply did not disclose it. However, we consider this unlikely.

Table 5.2 Ten most commonly mentioned factors and their specification

The name of the circumstance	*Number*	*% specified*
Previous convictions	144	82.6
Acknowledgment and cooperation	96	89.6
No criminal history	63	79.4
Committed during an operational period of a suspended prison sentence	50	88
Regret	36	94.44
Committal of more offences	28	89.3
Restitution of damages	27	88.9
Effectiveness of previous sentences	21	81
Personal circumstances in general	21	90.5
Offence on a larger scale, affecting more things or more people, or committed or continued for a longer period of time	17	70.6

Communication and formulation of principles

The role of appellate courts lies in correcting excesses and in contributing to consistent decision-making. Appellate courts can increase the consistency of future decisions in two ways. Firstly, appellate courts discuss the strength of an individual factor and implicitly or explicitly show what role it should (or should not) play. The way in which individual factors – acquiring various forms in specific cases – might influence sentence imposition can be explained, ideally by showing how the factor was misapplied. Secondly, appellate courts might – at times – generalise their findings and outline more general rules. Guideline judgments issued especially in the 1980s and 1990s in England and Wales, Australia and New Zealand are extreme examples of such generalisations, but the practice of appellate courts generalising the rules was commonly accepted in common-law jurisdictions even before this period (Freiberg & Sallmann, 2008).

We thus first investigate whether appellate courts convey their different perspectives on certain factors to first-level courts. Such an explanation is necessary so that first-level courts are persuaded and so that they follow an appellate court's opinion in future similar cases. However, in the majority of cases (53.8%), appellate courts did not enter into any conversation with first-level courts. In an additional 23.3% of cases, appellate courts only mentioned what the correct solution was, but did not explain why they disagreed with first-level courts. In the remaining 22.9% of cases, appellate courts mentioned both what the correct solution was and explained why they disagreed with first-level courts. Appellate courts, therefore, do not presently seize the opportunity to communicate what first-level courts should do better in relation to individual factors. This makes it difficult for first-level courts to learn from what appellate courts do.

We do not solely blame the appellate courts; due to the low level of justification provided by first-level courts, the appellate courts are often left guessing why the first-level courts decided the way they did. This greatly complicates the appellate courts' mission to debate with the first-level courts and explain what they did incorrectly. We understand the call to "pity the poor appellate judge" (Chanenson, 2006). Regardless of whose fault it is, first-level courts can learn little from the consideration of individual factors by appellate courts and typically have to infer these factors for themselves.

We then examined how often and in what ways appellate courts generalised their findings. General rules can play a greater role in unifying judicial decision-making, contributing to a sentencing jurisprudence. While not frequent, the formulations of such rules were not rare either; Czech appellate courts discussed them in 8.6% of cases. These rules touched on various sentencing issues: deciding on what type of punishment is appropriate, the length of sentences, the role of individual factors and their importance. Having elaborated them in detail elsewhere (Vanča & Drápal, 2023), we primarily discuss their quality below.

The fundamental issue which we identified is that these rules are not formulated following a coherent theory but are determined on an ad hoc basis by appellate judges who (evidently) prefer different sentence rationales and have different approaches to sentencing in general. To provide an example, an appellate court declared a suspended prison sentence to be insufficient if an offender caused the death of another person while under influence.[14] Although questionable (for example because offence-seriousness should not play a role in suspending a prison sentence in Czechia, see (Drápal, 2022a)), such a decision strongly emphasises the principle of proportionality. On the other hand, proportionality was clearly disregarded in two decisions in which appellate courts mentioned that offenders with a significant criminal history should be imposed sentences in the middle of a sentencing range.[15] Similarly, there was no discussion of proportionality when an appellate court determined that high age should play a mitigating role when imposing a sentence.[16] All of these results are questionable as they are, and their foundations contradict themselves. This isn't to suggest that all rules set by appellate courts were improper; some were reasonable. Yet, many did not contribute to a belief in a coherent sentencing jurisprudence.

14 Decision of the Regional Court in Brno sp. stamp 5 To 197/2016 of June 16, 2016.

15 Decision of the Regional Court in Pilsen sp. stamp 8 To 190/2016 of June 2, 2016; Decision of the Regional Court in Pilsen sp. stamp 7 To 362/2016 of September 22, 2016.

16 Decision of the Municipal Court in Prague sp. stamp 5 To 132/2016 of June 6, 2016.

We thus conclude that appellate courts cannot create a truly principled complex sentencing system without a complex sentencing framework and academic support that is currently missing in Central and Eastern Europe (Drápal & Plesničar, 2023). We reach a similar conclusion to Ashworth when discussing the role of appellate courts in England and Wales, where, due to the lack of any overall strategy, many frequent offences were not discussed in guideline judgments (Ashworth, 2009). Although our conclusions are similar, the mechanisms differ – no complex sentencing framework guiding appellate courts vs. no overall strategy – and thus require different solutions if the systems want appellate review to provide more guidance to sentencers.

Conclusion: broad unstructured discretion prevents the creation of sentencing jurisprudence

The Czech sentencing system currently provides judges with broad discretion. This offers a perfect opportunity for appellate courts to guide first-level courts and to develop a principled sentencing jurisprudence. However, this opportunity has not been realised, contrary to overly optimistic sentencing scholarship (Labbe, 1977) or theory (O'Malley, 2011, p. 115). In our opinion, the main reason for this is that the discretion is so broad that a detailed sentencing framework is missing and the sentencing process is unstructured. As a result, first-level courts struggle to give appellate courts a chance to review the sentencing process and make it difficult for appellate courts to develop a coherent, principled sentencing jurisprudence.

Thus, in order for appellate courts to develop a complex principled sentencing jurisprudence, several conditions need to be fulfilled:

- The statutory framework needs to be coherent and to enable just sentencing. Judges cannot (or at least should not) decide outside the law, and the law should outline the guiding principles of the sentencing framework (Rosenbaum, 2013). Appellate courts should generally not set sentencing policy; this is the responsibility of a different governmental branch (Freiberg & Sallmann, 2008) that should accept it.
- The sentencing process needs to be structured (Freiberg & Sallmann, 2008), which is impossible without specifying sentencing rationales (see Chapter 7). Thus, the sentencing framework is not sufficiently elaborated.
- Academia should offer guidance to appellate courts beyond a statutory sentencing framework; one cannot realistically expect non-English appellate judges to read books published by Oxford University Press and Hart on the role of previous convictions to decide which approach they prefer. Academia in individual countries should provide sufficient guidance.

- In the case of multiple appellate courts, their decision-making needs to be unified, typically by the Supreme Court. For example, there are ten Czech appellate courts (as well as several chambers within each, deciding independently of each other; some processes may have been different over time; similarly, see O'Malley, 2011, pp. 118–120). If we aim for consistent jurisprudence both within and between appellate courts' constituencies, one can hardly imagine it without the Supreme Court ruling on the most important questions and principles. The Supreme Court's role should be limited to a review of principles (not evidence) and could be achieved in different ways, either by ruling in individual cases or by delivering unifying opinions which should be issued if lower courts decide inconsistently (Drápal & Plesničar, 2023).

Given that these conditions are fulfilled, we believe that an appellate procedure might – at least several years later – result in a coherent principled sentencing jurisprudence. Without this, we are doubtful that appellate courts can provide detailed guidance to first-level courts. For 30 years, Czech appellate courts were left undisturbed; during this period, they might have come up with sentencing jurisprudence. Yet, our findings suggest that simply allowing appellate courts to rule (even rather broadly) on sentence principles does not result in a creation of a coherent principled sentencing jurisprudence. Such an approach instead results in excesses being – mostly – corrected, but these excesses are identified primarily via judicial experience and are not based on thorough deliberation or coherent principles. Consequently, some excesses might be overlooked while some sentences that are not excessive could be changed. First-level judges are thus made aware only of gross misapplications of sentencing principles, and appellate courts thus reduce the discretion offered to first-level judges only to a small extent. While this appellate review is useful, it plays only a limited role and cannot act as the decisive force contributing to a consistent sentencing.

The insufficient level of justifying sentencing by both first-level and appellate courts should also be acknowledged by international courts. In December 2023, the European Court for Human Rights (ECHR) ruled that, because an appellate court did not carefully scrutinise all relevant factors related to the case, the European Convention for Human Rights (art. 3 and 8) was violated.[17] Specifically, the appellate court suspended a prison sentence imposed by the first-level court, mentioning one factor while omitting other factors. This ECHR decision is strange, because – as we have demonstrated above – appellate courts almost never mention offence-related factors; thus, all such decisions should be overturned (which would be both impossible and inop-

17 Case of Vučković v. Croatia n. 15798/20, judgment issued on 12 December 2023.

portune). The reason behind the ECHR decision is likely dissatisfaction with the sentence imposed for rape; yet, the approach of ECHR is oversimplified, and it stems from typical legal views of appellate review, as it fails to reflect both the legal reality and the difficulties that the appellate review faces. We will find out in the future whether ECHR will begin to overturn cases because appellate courts mentioned only a few factors; in such cases, almost all Czech appellate decisions would have to be overturned, (probably) along with the decisions of most other appellate courts in Europe.

Limited retributivist appellate review

We conclude by proposing principles for an appellate system that might operate within a limited retributivist framework (Frase, 2012; von Hirsch, 2017). Such an approach would emphasise the prevention of disproportionately high sentences rather than the prevention of disproportionately low sentences and would provide more detailed guidance on assessing factors related to proportionality than other factors. The approach is based on a liberal tradition of mistrusting penal power stemming from its misuses in the past.

In order to realise a limited retributivist appellate review, judges would need to clearly say what sentence is proportionate to offence seriousness – or, in the words of Chapter 7, what is the provisional prison sentence set in Step 1. This provisional prison sentence could be identified by appellate courts even if first-level courts would not clearly define it, as it is largely offence-based. If a first-level court would impose a harsher sentence than what the appellate court would deem proportionate, the appellate court would have to interfere, even if it would require the sentence to be lowered by several days or weeks. By explaining how appellate courts consider offence seriousness, appellate courts would provide detailed guidance to first-level courts on principles upon which the sentencing system is founded. Appellate review would thus be designed to strengthen the core principles of the sentencing system.

If the first-level court imposed a more lenient sentence than a proportionate sentence, as considered by an appellate court, we argue that a significant disproportion would be necessary to impose a harsher sentence. This would mean that the provided guidance, in explaining which factors should reflect offence seriousness and in what way, will favour factors leading to the imposition of more lenient sentences over those leading to harsher sentences. We find this consequence apt, as we are more distrustful of the overuse of penal power than its underuse. Other issues than proportionality (e.g., inappropriate sentence type or consideration of previous convictions) would also require a higher standard of proof, such as significant inappropriateness or unreasonableness.

Ideally, these conclusions would result from a review of the process, not of the outcome. We hope that appellate courts might be less reluctant to say that a slightly less or more lenient sentence might have been imposed due to previous convictions playing too little or too significant a role, if at the same time they would specify that the imposed sentence is proportionate to the offender's behaviour. Although problematic, if the process could not be reviewed (or appellate courts would not divulge their assessment of it), but only the outcome would be reviewed, it would not necessarily prevent guidance regarding proportionality being offered. Factors relating to offence seriousness would be developed given the standard of review if an appellate court considered a proportionate sentence to be only slightly lower than the one imposed by a first-level court, while factors relating to other issues would not be properly developed. While not ideal, this could be acceptable in a system emphasising proportionality.

Such an approach would not necessarily encourage defendants to file appeals "just to try it" in large numbers. While defendants might appeal when proportionality is an issue, the higher standard of review relating to other issues might discourage some defendants from appealing.

Depending upon the preferences of each country, a similar emphasis could be placed on other types of decisions similar to that on proportionality. For example, if a system considered a prison sentence to be the sentence of last resort (presumption against imposition of a prison sentence), the custodial threshold in such a system could be enforced with similar strictness; if a prison sentence were imposed, appellate courts would have to change the sentence, even though a prison sentence could be a reasonable and appropriate option in such a case, and although it would not be the only option, and thus not a necessary decision.

The sentencing framework and preferred sentencing process should be reflected in how sentence imposition is justified and reviewed. Regarding the method of review, we find it more appropriate for an appellate court to review primarily the appropriateness of first-level courts' argumentation: consideration of all factors, their specification based on provided evidence, determination of factors' importance and the weighing of factors. Throughout this review, the appellate court could simply point out errors in the reasoning of the first-instance court, thereby contributing to a more detailed analysis of the principles of sentencing. Dividing the sentencing process into parts relating to different sentencing rationales would further enable appellate courts to apply varying standards of review to different decisions, reflecting the hierarchy of sentencing rationales and the preferences expressed by offenders. We will further demonstrate this point in Chapter 7. Yet prior to discussing it, we discuss experiences of one country that has attempted to improve sentence justification over the last decades: the Netherlands.

6 A review of sentence justification

The case of the Netherlands

Sonja Meijer

Introduction

Previous chapters have identified the low quality of sentence justification provided by both first instance and appellate courts. Given the importance of sentence justification, it is natural to deliberate about mechanisms that would improve its quality. This chapter presents the development of approaches to sentence justification in the Netherlands and various initiatives which have been taken to improve it. It is argued that in terms of enhancing sentence justification, two approaches can be taken. On the one hand, a top-down change is possible through the law by the legislator or the jurisprudence of a higher authority (Supreme Court). Which of the two approaches is successful depends heavily on how the sentence justification is regulated. In this chapter, the Netherlands will serve as a case study. It is illustrated that a top-down approach is unsuccessful for the case of the Netherlands due to a lack of sentencing rules in the law and the fact that the Dutch Supreme Court is not willing to impose stricter requirements on the sentencing justifications of first instance and appellate courts. It is noted that these conclusions may be different for other countries where, for example, a comprehensive regulation of sentencing and sentence justification is laid down in the law. Although the Netherlands is not a post-communist country, it is likely the only country that developed and tested multiple approaches to enhancing the quality of sentence justification. Dutch experiences are thus beneficial for anyone thinking about improving the quality of sentence justification, including the post-communist region. The aim of this chapter is thus to describe what efforts have been taken in the Netherlands to improve sentencing motivation, to highlight what is needed to improve sentencing justifications and by what routes this could be achieved.

After a short outline of the general legal framework and the ways in which sentencing discretion is structured in the Netherlands, it discusses the legal provisions and jurisprudence of the Supreme Court relating to sentence justification. Attempts from both within and outside of the judiciary to improve sentence justification bottom-up are examined next, with a specific focus being

DOI: 10.4324/9781003470670-6

given to the "Promis" project (Project on Improving Sentencing Justification) and the Committee on the Unity of Law, whose role it was to improve the explanation of the verdict. Given that the quality of sentence justification has not reached a sufficient level of quality, the last part of the chapter presents recent proposals on how sentence justification could be further improved and possible reasons for this failure.

From inequality to consistency of punishment and comprehensibility of the justification

The Netherlands does not have a sentencing tradition, as is the case with other countries (Schuyt, 2010). The discussion around sentencing previously focused mainly on the inequality of punishment, but since the 1990s more emphasis has been given to the consistency of punishment (Beaujean, 2008, 2012, 2014; Duker, 2003; Schoep, 2008). Inconsistent sentencing can lead to arbitrary punishment, which jeopardises the legitimacy of the sentence and the sentencing judge. Since the 1990s, instruments have been developed within the judiciary to ensure greater consistency in sentencing (Beaujean, 2012; Dijkstra, 1998; Schoep & Schuyt, 2005). Gradually, however, attention is also being paid to the intelligibility of the penalty decision and the sentence justification. More than in the past, judges are today expected to make their reasons explicit for choosing a certain sentence and level of punishment (Schuyt, 2010).

There are good reasons for this development. Research shows that a more understandable motivation for sentencing leads to greater acceptance of the criminal sentence. Explicitly mentioning the objectives of punishment in the motivation for sentencing will make sentencing justifications not only more convincing but also more understandable. According to the information thesis, more information about the criminal case leads to greater acceptance of the sentence and thus to a smaller punitivity gap, meaning the difference in the severity of the sentence that judges and the public (on average) consider appropriate (Elffers, 2017; Van der Schaaf & Malsch, 2015). Research carried out by Ernst (2020) also shows that greater sentencing justification leads to more understanding and greater acceptance of criminal sentences. On average, a justification for punishment which is of better quality, based on objective criteria, ensures more understanding and greater acceptance among those who take note of it, showing that there is a positive correlation between understanding and acceptance. In line with the information thesis, Ernst concludes that the better a punishment is motivated, and therefore the more information people have about it, the better the punishment is accepted.

The aim of this chapter is to describe what efforts have been taken in the Netherlands to improve sentencing motivation, to highlight what is needed to improve sentencing justifications and to consider by what routes this could be achieved. Given the fact that little has been written on sentencing justifications in international literature, this chapter also aims to provide insights into what works (and does not) in the Netherlands in this regard.[1]

The current sentencing framework

The legal framework

The Dutch sentencing system is presently characterised by a broad sentencing discretion for the judge and therefore a high degree of confidence in the judge's powers. The Dutch Criminal Code (CC) does not contain extensive rules on sentencing law. When imposing the sentence, the judge has the choice between the type of sanction (penalty or measure) and the modality (conditional or unconditional). Regarding the level of punishment (the duration or the amount), the Criminal Code provides for a general minimum penalty and a general maximum penalty. The term of imprisonment is defined as not less than one day and not more than 30 years (Art. 10 CC). In addition to the prison sentence, the code also provides for a life sentence. As far as the fine is concerned, a minimum of €3 and a maximum of €1,030,000 is set (Art. 23 CC). The law does not provide for minimum penalties for each offence, but it does provide for maximum penalties for each offence, that is, the maximum penalty that is regulated by law for each offence. For example, simple assault carries a maximum sentence of 3 years, and manslaughter carries a prison sentence of 25 years. The court is bound by these statutory minimums and maximums but is virtually free within these limits. The judge can also apply the judicial pardon: the finding of guilt without the imposition of a penalty (Art. 9a CC).

The judge's discretion in sentencing has been restricted by the legislature only in several cases. The possibility of accumulation is limited only in a few cases. For example, the court may not impose a prison sentence of more than 6 months in combination with community service (Art. 9(4) CC). Furthermore, in certain cases, it is not permitted to impose community service (Art. 22b CC). This is the case, for example, with a conviction for an offence which is punishable by a term of imprisonment of 6 years or more and if the offence has seriously offended the physical integrity of the victim. This is also the case with certain sexual offences, where the defendant has previously been convicted of community service in the 5 years preceding the offence and has performed that community service, or when he did not perform this community service and he was ordered to be in substitute

1 Parts of this chapter are based on the research that has been carried out in the context of the Changing Justice Gears project, which I will elaborate on below (Meijer et al., 2021).

custody. Incidentally, it is possible to deviate from this regulation in the sense that community service can be imposed in combination with one day of unconditional imprisonment, a possibility that is regularly used in practice (De Ridder et al., 2018). In addition, a prison sentence of more than 2 years cannot be imposed entirely conditionally, and a prison sentence of 4 years cannot be imposed partially conditionally (art. 14 CC). Further, in the event of an attempt, the maximum main penalty is reduced by one-third (art. 45 para 2 CC).

Sentencing guidelines

Both judges and the prosecution service have their own guidelines for determining sentencing and sentencing decisions. The *Landelijk Overleg Vakinhoud Strafrecht* (LOVS) of the *Raad voor de rechtspraak* (Judiciary Council) publishes so-called guidelines for sentencing by judges with the aim of achieving a consistent national sentencing policy. In the case of frequently occurring offences, a level of punishment (orientation point) is given which the judge can keep in mind when imposing the sentence. The landmarks reflect the punishment that judges usually impose for the most common manifestation of the offence.[2] The landmarks are therefore a representation of practice and are explicitly not intended to guide that practice (Lensing, 2021). The guidelines are established by the LOVS on the proposal of the *Commissie Rechtseenheid* (Committee on the Unity of Law) after an inventory of the practice of sentencing and after consultation with all courts (Beaujean, 2012).

Judges are not bound by the landmarks. According to the settled case law of the Supreme Court, the landmarks cannot be regarded as law within the scope of Article 79 of the Judicial Organisation Act (*Wet op de Rechterlijke Organisatie*, RO).[3] The rationale for this is that the landmarks referred to do not originate from a body that has the power to bind judges.

Sentencing guidelines (*Strafvorderingsrichtlijnen*) for public prosecutors come from the Board of Procurators General of the Public Prosecution Service and are countersigned by the Minister of Justice and Security. The criminal procedure guidelines are therefore law within the scope of Section 79 of the RO Act because they originate from an authority that has the power to prescribe binding rules to the various parts of the Public Prosecutor's Office. This means, for example, that lawyers can rely on the principles formulated in the Sentencing Guidelines in criminal proceedings and that the public prosecutor must justify any deviations from them.

2 https://www.rechtspraak.nl/sitecollectiondocuments/orientatiepunten-en-afspraken-lovs.pdf.

3 Supreme Court 3 December 2002, NJ 2003, 570 and Supreme Court 31 January 2017, ECLI:NL:HR:2017:114

The reasons for the sentencing decision

Sentence justifications under Article 359(6) of the Code of Criminal Procedure

Article 359(5) of the Code of Criminal Procedure (CCP) prescribes that the judgment must state the reasons that determined the sentence or led to the measure. Regarding unconditional custodial sentences and measures involving deprivation of liberty, the sixth paragraph of Article 359 CCP contains a special obligation to state the reasons that led to the choice of this type of penalty or this type of measure. In addition, the judgment must indicate, as far as possible, what has been considered in determining the length of the sentence.

By including the very briefly formulated obligation to state the reasons of Article 359(6) CCP, the Committee on Financial Sanctions (*Commissie Vermogenssancties*) tried to reduce the short prison sentence. When the Penal Code was introduced in 1886, a strong emphasis was given to imprisonment as the main punishment for crimes. Following the recommendations of the Committee on Financial Sanctions (Interim Report on Property Penalties 1969), the Asset Sanctions Act (*Wet vermogenssancties*) (Act of 31 March 1983, Official Journal 1983, No 153) made it possible to impose a fine for each offence. Although the Financial Sanctions Act aimed to reduce the short prison sentence, the legislator's desire for doing this was much less motivated in principle than that of the Financial Sanctions Committee. The capacity problems that had arisen in the prison system played an especially important role in the discussion.[4]

The intended aim has been recognised in criminal procedural law by the inclusion of an increased requirement to state the reasons in what is now Article 359(6) CCP. It was noted that the existing obligation to state the reasons (the current Article 359(5) CCP) in practice leads to very brief justifications ("in view of the seriousness of the offence, the circumstances under which the offence was committed and the person of the perpetrator"). The legislator expressed the hope that the new wording of Article 359 CCP will ensure "that in future the judge will deliberate even more than at present on the question of why he imposes a certain sentence and not another and furthermore that he will record his reasons in the judgment in a way that is as clear as possible for the convicted person."[5] Moreover, the judgment should contain not only the specific reasons which led to the decision to impose a custodial sentence, but also, as far as possible, the circumstances considered in determining the length of the sentence. At the same time, it was noted that it cannot be expected that "it will be possible to explain in a criminal judgment

4 Parliamentary Papers II 1977/78, 15 012, no. 3, p. 19.
5 Parliamentary Papers II 1977/78, 15 012, nos. 1–3, p. 37, 54–55.

with mathematical accuracy why a certain type of penalty and a certain level of punishment has been chosen and no other."[6]

More than four decades later, we can conclude that the provision has not had the desired effect of the legislator. The current requirements for the statement of reasons do not lead to satisfactory justifications that provide insight into the considerations of the criminal court for opting for a certain sentencing over another (e.g. Claessen & Meijer, 2022; De Hullu, 2002). Regarding short prison sentences, it is also important that the reasons for this are usually not put into writing. Short prison sentences can also be imposed by a single judge who is competent to try simple cases and impose prison sentences of up to one year (art. 369(2) CCP). Usually, immediately after the conclusion of the investigation, the court issues an oral judgment at the hearing (Article 378(1) CCP), which makes it impossible to verify afterwards whether the court complied with the increased obligation to state reasons.

Case law on the criminal court's obligation to provide sentence justifications

In the case law of the Supreme Court, the above-mentioned requirement to state the reasons on the basis of Article 359(6) CCP is interpreted in such a way that "it must be explicitly clear from the sentence justification that the court has taken into account the fact that it is imposing a penalty or measure that entails unconditional deprivation of liberty by expressing in the sentence justification and by linking that imposition of the sanction to the reasons stated in sentence justification" (Supreme Court 27 September 2016, ECLI:NL:HR:2016:2191). A general consideration of the nature and seriousness of the proven offences, the circumstances under which they were committed and the person of the suspect is insufficient (Supreme Court 9 February 2021, ECLI:NL:HR:2021:165, 166 and 167). A mere reference to the circumstances of the case and the extract from the defendant's judicial documentation showing that he has previously been convicted of similar offences is also not sufficient (Supreme Court 9 February 2021, ECLI:NL:HR:2021:164). However, this requirement is met if the court includes considerations in the judgment regarding the seriousness of the offence, a previous conviction for a similar offence and the LOVS landmarks (Supreme Court 27 September 2016, ECLI:NL:HR:2016:2191). The bar is not set very high.

Currently the court is free to select and evaluate factors that led to the imposition of a sentence. The judge is also not obliged to give reasons for this selection (Supreme Court 26 June 1984, NJ 1985, 138 and Supreme Court 16 November 1999, *NJ* 2000, 214). Further reasoning is only required

6 Parliamentary Papers II 1977/78, 15 012, no. 3, p. 37

if the defense has put forward an explicitly substantiated position (Article 359a CCP) with regard to the imposition of the sentence, if the imposed sentence is surprising or if the sentence is incomprehensible (Supreme Court 2 June 2009, ECLI:NL:HR:2009:BH8313 and Supreme Court 3 October 2006, ECLI:NL:HR:2006:AX5479).

Currently the bar for the success of a cassation appeal relating to the unsubstantiated disregard of positions on the reasons for the sentence is high. The main argument for this is that, according to the Supreme Court, the abovementioned broad discretion for judges with regard to sentencing "*prevents the Supreme Court from imposing excessive, generally formulated requirements on the court's duty to respond to sentencing defences.*" Furthermore, "*it is the court on the merits that bears the important responsibility to assess in which specific cases it is desirable to give the defendant, any victims and/or the public insight into the special reasons for the punishment by means of a sentencing consideration tailored to the case.*"[7]

Janssen, Kuster and Paridaens (2017) deduce from this that the Supreme Court wants to place the motivation for sentencing mainly in the hands of the court and that it is important that courts take this responsibility. However, I agree with Fokkens (2019) that it is not clear why the judge's discretion in sentencing would prevent the Supreme Court from setting high, generally formulated requirements concerning their duty to respond to sentencing defences. According to the legislative history outlined above, the legislature clearly took a different view, and the judge's obligation to state the reasons in response to sentencing defences does not seem to limit the criminal court's own responsibility for sentencing in any way. An obligation to respond is more work, but that is another matter for assessing the judge's discretion in sentencing. However, the Supreme Court case law discussed above illustrates that a top-down approach in improving sentencing motivations, in the sense that the Supreme Court imposes stricter requirements on the sentencing motivations of courts, is ruled out.

Attempts within the judiciary to improve sentence justification

Over the years, various attempts have been made, both within and outside the judiciary, to improve the way in which sentencing is justified, with particular emphasis on its explicatory function and, to a lesser extent, on the desire to achieve consistent sentencing. The following two sections discuss, in chronological order, two main projects that aimed to improve sentencing motivation

7 https://www.rechtspraak.nl/Organisatie-en-contact/Organisatie/Hoge-Raad-der-Nederlanden/Over-de-Hoge-Raad/Publicaties/Documents/HR%20jaarverslag%202015.pdf.

which have been developed within the judiciary. The last section then discusses three proposals by academics.

Promis

Within the judicial system, the desire to arrive at more comprehensible reasons for punishment has taken shape in the Promis project (Project Motiveringsverbetering in Strafvonnissen or Project on Improving Sentencing Justification). This project has been (and still is) the most important bottom-up approach to enhancing sentence justification in the Netherlands. The purpose of a Promis judgment is to arrive at better evidentiary reasoning and sentence justification, so that improved communication is established between the criminal court, the counsel, other parties involved and society. In this way, the sentence justification is hoped to provide better insight into the judge's thought process.[8] In this project, the reasoning for the evidence of the criminal act has received particular attention, but not much attention has been paid to the sentence justification (De Groot-van Leeuwen et al., 2015).

The elements from the evidentiary and sentencing model developed in the Promis project contain the following list of elements regarding the statement of reasons for the penalty:

- A short, readable description of the facts;
- The facts that the public prosecutor deems proven, and the punishment demanded for them;
- The position of the defence;
- Any (partial) acquittals in the first instance;
- The punishment imposed in similar cases (landmark; not mandatory);
- Statutory justification for penalties and measures;
- Further justification for penalties and measures arising from positions explicitly substantiated by the defence or the Public Prosecution Service, the debate at the hearing or the jurisprudential requirements for reasoning;
- Fact-related factors, the impact of the offence with a list of general and specifically objective factors that affect the sanction assessment; and
- Suspect-related factors with a list of subjective factors that influence the sentencing.

This model is not applied by all courts and tribunals. One of the weaknesses of this model is that no position is taken regarding the question of what should be taken as a starting point: a LOVS landmark or a landmark of the court itself.

8 Final Report Pilot Promis 2005.

However, there seems to be consensus that it is less appropriate to take the prosecutor's point of view as a starting point. Moreover, there is no obligation for the judge to substantiate in his reasons any deviations from the first instance verdict. This would be advisable, as in this way the judge provides more insights into his reasoning, and the sentencing motivation gains greater persuasiveness.[9]

Criticisms of the Promis model have also been expressed. Based on a systematic comparison of criminal justifications before and after the Promis project, Van den Hoven and Plug (2009) conclude that Promis has led to an improvement in the motivation of the sentence, but that the instrument of the Promis reasoning is inadequate. In their view, the model presented in the Promis project for an intelligible sentence justification does not show the argumentative structure that the elements should form altogether. The model is a list of elements, but the relationship between the elements is not made explicit. Nor is the underlying theoretical analysis sufficient. The model is not based on a theory about what an adequate motivation for punishment should be. As a result, the punishment is rarely clearly motivated; the description of the offences (A) is often separate from the sentencing. The facts that the public prosecutor deems proven, the punishment demanded for them (B) and the position of the defence (C) are often inserted into the reasons without a function. The landmarks (E) are given, but not because there is an alternative.

According to Van den Hoven and Plug, the model suggests an ideal, namely that a full justification of the type and duration of the punishment can and should be formulated. When that ideal turns out not to be achievable, however, it leads to a "blurring" application among the individual users of the model; some keep to the order of the model and do not use an argumentation structure, some try to develop an argumentation structure and leave the order of the model for what it is and some try to use the order of the model and also develop an argument which leads to a lot of repetition (Van den Hoven & Plug, 2009).

Van den Hoven and Plug formulate several recommendations. They write:

> First, the theory behind a Decision and Punishment Justification model needs to be thought through. What is an adequate and feasible justification for punishment? Can the duration of the sentence be justified consistently in relation to appealing standard cases (the landmarks)? Can the court justify a possible deviation from the Public Prosecution Service (as the voice of society) and how convincing and informative is that for society? To what extent can the court provide insightful justification for why it is relatively high or low in a case on the scale of possible sentences, how

9 Report of the Promis Review Committee III, State of affairs of Promis in 2010 and Report of the Review Committee, Final Report of Promis II.

exactly does it pretend to be able to do so? What is at least a standard set of recognizable criteria that reduce and aggravate penalties, and what is a good formulation of those criteria? And above all: how do the various elements fit into a clear argumentation structure which, it should be clear, must necessarily be built from the category – the criteria – which is now completely missing!

The evaluation study "The Verdict Better Explained" by De Groot-van Leeuwen, Laemers and Sportel (2015) presents a similar picture. As far as the intelligibility of the statement of reasons for the statement of evidence is concerned, the authors concluded that it has improved considerably in recent years. However, the justification for the motivation for the penalty often offers little insight. The criminal court's reasoning about the type and degree of punishment is only briefly discussed in the judgment. It is unclear, for example, why a sentence of a certain duration is imposed and why community service is imposed and not a prison sentence or vice versa. They conclude that Promis judgments do not offer much more insight in this respect than classical judgments.

The central question in these authors' evaluation study is whether the introduction of Promis has led to more acceptance, in addition to a more understandable justification. To assess the acceptance of the type of sentence, the respondents were asked what punishment the court imposed and what punishment they would have given themselves. The study shows no significant difference in the type of sentence between people who read a classic judgment and people who read a Promis judgment. According to De Groot-van Leeuwen, Laemers and Sportel, this can be explained by the fact that, although the Promis judgments contain more information about the offence and the finding of provenance, the justifications for the type of sentence do not differ very much from the classic criminal judgments. As far as the level of punishment is concerned, the authors do note significant differences between Promis sentences and classic sentences. In the case of the Promis judgments, respondents were significantly more likely to agree with the court than in the case of traditional judgments, which, according to them, can be explained by the fact that more information about the court's reasoning – in this case, the relative size of the sentence and aggravating and mitigating circumstances – leads to more agreement with the court.

Committee on the Unity of Law

The second most well-known bottom-up approach to enhancing the sentence justification in the Netherlands has been a project of the Committee for the Unity of Law, which was established in 2015. Partly because of the evaluation study mentioned above, the LOVS set up this committee with the intention of better explaining the verdict. The reason for setting up this committee was, on the one hand, the importance of the motivation for the sentence, the defendant, the victim and other participants in the proceedings; and, on the other hand, the importance of the sentencing reasons for the judge's discretion in sentencing, which has come under pressure in recent years due to ambiguities that regularly arise in sentencing. The task of this committee was as follows (Janssen et al., 2017):

> to see whether the criminal court can be given tools to make the sentencing justification clearer, whereby the LOVS draws particular attention to the objectives of sentences, the aggravating and mitigating circumstances, the role of participation, attempt and preparation in sentencing, concurrence, recidivism, procedural grounds for reduced sentence, and the influence of the defendant's attitude on the sentencing.

The Committee took a broad approach to its task and examined both the substantive side of the sentencing motivation and the communicative side (Klijn, 2017). The committee took the guidelines for sentencing as a starting point. These offer "a beginning of thought." The landmarks are based on what is customarily imposed for such a crime by courts and tribunals and are therefore descriptive and prescriptive in this sense. The legitimacy of the landmarks therefore lies in a lengthy and consistent sentencing by courts and tribunals.

The Committee presented the results of the project to the LOVS. Specifically, it presented a sentencing model that is partly based on Schuyt's model (see Chapter 3) and which consists of three elements:

> the factors that we know, the valuation, (the weight) of those factors and, finally, the weighing of the mutual relationship between the named factors. The factors we know include, for example, the nature of the offence (protected legal interest), what exactly happened (modus operandi, premeditated, degree of culpability), consequences for the victim, survivors and society, the person of the suspect (first offender or repeat offender, the capacity, motive, remorse), the legal context in which the sentence is imposed (multiple concurrence, reasonable time, obligations to state reasons), the social context (the offence is directed against office holders or in the context of an event) and the relevant landmark. Subsequently, the evaluation of these factors takes place: do the factors increase or reduce the sentence? Finally, the weighing of the relationship between the factors mentioned follows. The punishment goals also play an important role in this, because based on them it can be made explicit what we intend to achieve with the punishment (in the words of the committee: 'retribution, general or special prevention or rehabilitation'). (Abbink, 2016)

Despite the committee's efforts, this proposal has not been followed up in practice.

Proposals from the legal profession

Proposals have also been made outside the judiciary to improve the accountability of sentencing. Schuyt's model can be seen as the first major proposal for improving punishment. This model is, like the two proposals to be discussed below, also a bottom-up approach with regard to enhancing the sentence justification. Since it is discussed in detail in Chapter 3, reference is made to that chapter. The other two proposals, the sentencing template of Elffers and the most recent attempt to improve the sentencing decision by the Changing Justice Gears project, are discussed below.

Elffers' sentencing template

Elffers (2016) emphasises that a justification for a sentence often comes down to a – in his view, rather obligatory – enumeration of facts and circumstances, but that this does not show how the ultimately imposed sentence relates to those considerations. He argues that judges should be explicit in how the enumeration of arguments leads to a certain sentence or to an increase or reduction of the sentence.

Elffers further contends that the sentencing paragraph in a judgment should be based on a sentencing template. This template has a fixed part, which goes through the various balancing points, and a variable part, which allows the court to consider the specific circumstances of the case. As the starting point of the template, Elffers takes the punishment proposed in the landmarks without arguing that the landmarks should be declared binding. Nor does he argue that the template should be mandatory. Considerations regarding the sentencing objectives do not appear in the idea for the proposed sentencing template. Perhaps a factor in this regard is that Elffers explicitly wants to leave the elaboration of the sentencing template to practice (a bottom-up approach); he calls for a working group of judges to make a somewhat more refined model and to experiment with it in simple cases.

The idea for the sentencing template has not been received with enthusiasm by the legal profession. One criticism is the lack of legal tools for sentencing. The current LOVS landmarks are a starting point for thinking, lack legal force and are also not generally accepted within the profession. By way of comparison, Tak points to the German system in which the judge must first determine a sentencing framework (Strafrahmen) – with corresponding minimum and maximum sentences – based on clear definitions laid down in the Penal Code. This sentencing framework is based on mandatory and optional penalty-increasing and penalty-reducing circumstances regulated by law. Within this established framework, the court must then indicate how it values them, using established criteria. Moreover, Tak notes that the "Dutch legal culture [characterised] by an excessively broad interpretation of judicial independence also plays a role." Janssen also calls the justification of sentencing "a sacred house": Dutch judges seem allergic to (too much) interference in "the real judicial work." At the same time, he acknowledges that there is broad support in the judiciary that "something" needs to be done in terms of sentencing motivation. In this regard, he points to the aforementioned attention that the Supreme Court called to in its 2015 annual report on sentencing and deduces from this that courts bear the greatest responsibility for a good justification of punishment.

Changing Justice Gears

Changing Justice Gears (CJG) focuses on reducing the short prison sentence (less than 6 months) that is relatively often imposed in the Netherlands. No less than 75% of all prison sentences in the Netherlands are shorter than 6 months. A key part of the project focuses on the motivation of the sentence, the conclusions of which I present below. The idea is that using (a model of) punishment goals for sentencing leads to improving punishment motivation. Improving sentence justification would then potentially lead to the less frequent imposition of short prison sentences and the more frequent imposition of alternatives to imprisonment.

As mentioned before, Article 359(6) CCP contains a special obligation to state the reasons that led to the choice of unconditional custodial sentences and measures involving deprivation of liberty. In addition, the judgment must indicate, as far as possible, what has been considered in determining the length of the sentence. In the current pending bill for the modernisation of the Code of Criminal Procedure, this special obligation is abolished.

CJG argues in favour of retaining this special obligation, because the abolition would mean that the principle of subsidiarity would disappear from the Code of Criminal Procedure. Moreover, the sentencing involves many questions that the judge should ideally answer, such as why he imposes a custodial sentence (and why not a lighter sanction), why a sentence lasts for a certain amount or duration, why this sentence is imposed on this defendant and so on. By requiring justification only if the sentencing is incomprehensible or surprising, as suggested, the legislator sends the signal that insight into the justification for the sentence is not necessary in most decisions imposing a custodial sentence. However, a better justification of the sentence provides insight into the judge's motives in imposing a certain sentence and, as mentioned above, ensures more understanding and greater acceptance of criminal sentences. This in turn promotes the legitimacy of sentencing and confidence in the judge. This will also prevent dissatisfaction with the penalties imposed, which may ultimately lead to calls from politicians and society more broadly for an increase in the maximum penalties or a restriction on the imposition of certain sanctions. It is argued that, in the absence of a statutory obligation to state reasons, it is up to the court to properly state reasons for sentencing. In this regard, CJG takes a bottom-up approach in terms of improving sentencing justification. The judge's broad discretion in sentencing entails a responsibility to provide insights into the judge's motives for imposing a particular sentence (Meijer et al., 2021).

CJG also argues that sentencing goals should be explicitly considered in the sentencing motivation. Specifically, it contends that a certain concept of sentencing goals should be laid down in the law, the LOVS landmarks and the criminal procedure guidelines of the Public Prosecution Service, which is a more top-down approach in terms of improving sentence justification. CJG argues that a certain ranking of sentencing goals is possible based on the principle of subsidiarity, which adhere to a certain order. Although in the Netherlands there is no hierarchy between penalty goals, this model still works with a ranking of penalty goals. The order of sentencing aims is based on the idea that the pursuit of some sanction objectives, such as rehabilitation, will lead to less drastic consequences for the offender (lighter sanctions), while the pursuit of other sanction objectives (general prevention and deterrence) will lead to more serious consequences (heavier sanctions). Using this particular ranking of sentencing aims encourages the court to think about the purpose for which it wants to impose a particular sanction. The hypothesis of this (ongoing) study is that this will lead to the imposition of short detentions less often.

In practice, as mentioned above, various attempts have been made to arrive at clearer sentencing justifications. It is debatable to what extent these attempts have contributed to an improvement in the justification of the sentence. There appears to have been no follow up by the judiciary to the (bottom-up) efforts of the working groups to improve the motivation of sentencing. However, the view that "something" should be done about the motivation for sentencing seems to be widely supported in legal practice. At the same time, it should be noted that the motivation for the penalty is a sensitive issue in practice. There is a fear that further provisions on the motivation of the sentence will lead to restriction of the judge's discretion to impose sentences, although it is (rightly) pointed out that higher requirements for the explication do not necessarily mean a restriction of this freedom (Klijn, 2017). On the contrary, the identification of sentencing objectives can make court decisions more convincing and understandable, which contributes to the legitimation of sentencing reasons.

Concluding thoughts

This chapter has shown that there are good reasons to work on improving sentencing motivation. In this chapter, I have illustrated that, depending on how sentencing systems are designed, that in improving sentencing motivation, either a top-down approach or a bottom-up approach or a mix of both can be chosen. In a top-down approach, the legislature can prescribe detailed sentencing rules into legislation, forcing the judge to better motivate a sentence. In addition, the Supreme Court can rule on the sentencing motivation of first instance and appellate courts. In a bottom-up approach, however, change comes from the legal practice itself. Judges in this case are aware of the importance of good sentencing motivation.

Over recent decades in the Netherlands, various mostly bottom-up proposals have been developed to improve the sentencing decision and its justification. A pessimistic conclusion would be that none of these proposals has led to improvements in sentencing motivation in law or practice. CJG's research has shown that the motivation for the penalty is a sensitive issue in practice and that various bottlenecks stand in the way of actual improvements. These bottlenecks are related to three causes: (i) the provision of information, (ii) the culture among and attitude of judges and (iii) organisational limitations. Firstly, judges do not always have sufficient information to decide on sentencing, for example because the suspect is convicted in absentia and there is no information on the suspect. Secondly, judges fear that their discretion to impose sentences will be restricted, which means that they are very reluctant to give guidance regarding the motivation of the sentence. Moreover, the guidelines developed by the case law seem to stand in the way of innovation. They are a representation of practice but explicitly not a guide to that practice. Finally, it is also pointed out, among others by judges, that better and therefore more extensive motivation often takes more time, which is something that judges regularly lack.

A top-down change seems only possible through the law or the jurisprudence of a higher authority (Supreme Court). Both paths seem unsuccessful in the case of the Netherlands. It should be noted that this conclusion is specifically related to the legal regulation (or better said, lack thereof) of sentencing in the Netherlands. These conclusions may be different for other countries where, for example, the law has a comprehensive regulation of sentencing.

A more optimistic conclusion is that the view that "something" should be done with the justification for sentencing seems to be widely supported in legal practice. However, in the Netherlands, change must come from that practice (bottom-up). The success of proposals to improve sentencing motivations seems to depend largely on judicial culture and its willingness to change. When considering models to improve sentencing decisions, this is certainly an issue to be considered.

7 Towards proper sentence justification

Jakub Drápal

Introduction

As Chapters 4 and 5 have shown, to understand why courts – both first-level and appellate – impose certain sentences is difficult or even impossible. Some attempts have aimed at improving the situation, namely by providing a list of elements that should be mentioned in a decision, but this has proven to be insufficient, as Chapter 6 discussed. It is, however, crucial not to give up the development of measures destined to improve the quality of reasoning. This is not only for reasons relating to legitimacy, as discussed in Chapter 2, but also because reason-giving cannot be divorced from the way that courts decide if sentence justification is to reflect the actual reasons behind the decision. Improving reason-giving might thus improve sentence imposition.

The aim of this final chapter is to elaborate on the principles of a principled sentencing process that might be reflected in sentence justifications. Specifically, I employ the three stages of reason-giving as outlined in Chapter 3. Given that countries approach the sentencing process and principles differently, I do this while emphasising that sentence justification requirements are context-dependent.

The basic tenet of my proposal is that the sentencing process needs to be structured more specifically (as was also already suggested in Chapter 6). The majority of current sentencing systems direct judges to consider a large number of factors at the same time, without telling or explaining to them how to do so. In Czechia, for example, the law stipulates 70 factors which a court needs to take into account. Considering all these factors in a principled way is impossible – being too difficult to manage – if all factors are to be considered at the same time. Instead, consideration of such a large amount of factors needs to be divided into several steps, whereby judges successively decide on individual sentence elements based on selected factors. The sentencing process can be considered as the outcome of the steps which a judge needs to take, akin to a decision-making tree (similarly, instead of a sentencing process, one can think of it as a "sentencing protocol"). Such an approach is both recommended by organisational decision-making literature (Wright & Goodwin, 2008) and has been adopted in different forms by England and

DOI: 10.4324/9781003470670-7

Wales and Sweden (Jareborg & Žíla, 2022, Chapter 13; Sentencing Council, 2019), which are among the few countries which strongly deliberate over principled sentencing. Three levels of reasoning outlined in Chapter 3 – specifying, direction and importance and weighing – would need to be carried out within each step to ensure the comprehensibility of the decision taken at a specific step. Such structuring of a sentencing process would reveal the choices taken by sentencers, emphasising the consistency of approach (as opposed to the consistency of outcome), which is a preferred method of achieving consistency (Harris, 2022, pp. 25–32).

In this chapter, I discuss the sentencing steps which a judge needs to take to arrive at a principled sentence and provide an in-depth justification of this process. In outlying the individual steps, I have taken inspiration from both how the English and Welsh guidelines are structured and how Sweden structures the sentencing process. First, I argue that a structured process should differ across sentencing systems and suggest principles which should be common to systems, emphasising proportionality. After this, I specify an easily understandable process in a post-communist setting, specifically in Czechia. After a concise introduction to the system, I outline seven steps which Czech judges should take to be accountable for their decisions; in doing so, I discuss applications of these steps in systems different from the Czech one. I close the chapter by discussing how different criminal justice actors might contribute to a principled process, revealing why they decided specifically what they decided – in other words, how sentences were recommended by prosecutors, imposed by first-level judges and reviewed by appellate judges.

Principles of a (proportionate) sentencing process

Sentencing varies across countries. Most importantly, sentencing rationales, sentencing principles and types of sentences all differ. These different approaches to sentencing shape the sentencing process, making it impossible to design a one-size-fits-all solution. One of the most important distinctions lies in what sentencing rationales a system emphasises: should a process prioritise proportionality or utilitarian aims? If proportionality is the determining principle, (i) the penal value of the criminal behaviour will be determined at the beginning of a sentencing process, and judges will not be able to impose a harsher punishment than the one proportionate to this penal value; meanwhile (ii) the commensurability of sanctions[1] will be clearly defined so that punishment would be proportionate to the penal value. On the other hand, if utilitarian purposes are given primacy, the emphasis would be given to establishing offenders and victims' risks and needs, and judges would impose the most effective sentence. In this chapter, I adopt a proportionality paradigm, specifi-

1 That is, clearly expressed exchange ratios between different types of sanctions, e.g. how many day fines or hours of community service are equivalent to one day of imprisonment.

cally a limiting retributivist paradigm, to address the issue of how to properly impose sentences and provide reasons for it.

Selecting a primary rationale – proportionality – is not sufficient to outline the steps of a sentencing process. The emphasis placed on other rationales needs to be specified as well. This point can be best illustrated by taking the example of guilty pleas. In a resolutely proportional system, guilty pleas should not influence whether someone is imprisoned or not (Roberts & Dagan, 2023; Roberts & Harris, 2017). On the other hand, if a special emphasis is placed either on the effectiveness of an investigation or the offenders' rehabilitation, non-imprisonment solely due to a guilty plea should be possible. Before outlining the sentencing process, criminal justice systems' creators should thus clearly state not only what sentencing rationales they prioritise but also to what extent the primary rationale can be overridden.

The sentencing process will further differ in systems which emphasise similar rationales, since sentencing principles and the approaches of expressing them differ across countries. Multiple offending is a perfect example of this. Every country employs some kind of totality principle – providing a discount for multiple offenders (Ryberg et al., 2018) – yet there are different approaches to how it is done. In Germany, Slovenia and Sweden, for example, judges impose sentences for every offence (behaviour) individually and combine them into one final sentence. On the other hand, in, Austria, Czechia and Slovakia, judges impose sentences for all offences at once, without the mid-level step of imposing a sentence for each offence individually. The same issue might be resolved in common-law countries via concurrent or consecutive sentences. The sentencing process has to reflect these different approaches, although they might only consist of implementing sentencing principles.

Similarly, sanctions systems and preferences regarding the choice of a specific sanction type will shape the sentencing process. Is a suspended prison sentence considered a prison sentence or not? If yes, one must first decide whether a custodial threshold has been crossed and only then determine a suspension; if not, a different process is required. Likewise, the sentencing process will differ according to whether a non-suspended prison sentence is a sanction of last resort or whether it is considered one of several sanctions available in the arsenal of sanctions. Overall, the sentencing process needs to be constructed – at least to a certain extent – for each system individually.

Systems favouring proportionality would, however, approach the sentencing process similarly in some respects. Proportionality requires the construction of two scales: offence seriousness and sentence severity (von Hirsch, 2017, pp. 63–69). First, judges must determine the penal value of a sanctioned behaviour (Jareborg, 1994; Jareborg & Žíla, 2022, Chapter 13.3) that quantifies offences' seriousness. We do not discuss in this chapter whether this should be done using living standard analysis (von Hirsch & Jareborg, 1991), a discomfort index (Von Hirsch et al., 1989) or a different measure;

systems could also differ in this respect. The importance is that the offences' seriousness is quantified.

The ensuing question is what metric should be used to quantify it. Two primary options are a provisional prison sentence or an abstract scale (Robinson, 1994; Schiff, 1997; Tak, 2001). A prison sentence is, in my view, preferable,[2] since (i) it results in an imaginable scale; (ii) a prison sentence is, in many systems, the only sentence that can be imposed for all offences, the so-called universal sentence; and (iii) some judges are already considering sentence imposition in this way, especially when imposing intermediate sanctions. Although such an approach has a few disadvantages – such as a seeming preference for a prison sentence (Drápal, 2022c) – I consider the advantages to be more important.

The commensurability of different sentence types (sanctions' equivalence) needs to be defined to compare the severity of different sanction types. The prison sentence is not the only sentence which judges impose, and if the offences' seriousness is quantified using a provisional prison sentence, judges need to know upon imposing other sanction types how to transform the provisional prison sentence into an intermediate sentence of a specific length. Thus, a relationship between one day of imprisonment and the given hours of community sentence or number of day fines must be clearly specified. These ratios will be only an approximation, and they will result only in a rough equivalence of sanctions (Morris & Tonry, 1990, pp. 97–100; Robinson, 1994), but they are necessary to link a sanctioned behaviour's penal value to a sanction's penal bite. At this point I do not discuss what ratios are appropriate; they have been long studied using various methods (Pina-Sánchez et al., 2019; Sebba, 1978; Sebba & Nathan, 1984).

The easiest way to define relationships between different sentences is to consider ratios between sanctions following a breach or default, using prison sentence as a common currency. The law typically specifies how many unpaid fines, unperformed hours of community sentences or days of house arrest result in one day of imprisonment. While these ratios differ across systems (Drápal, 2018) and they might not be sufficiently thought through – such as one unpaid day fine resulting in two days of imprisonment, as is the case in Czechia – they are the ratios instituted by a legislator, providing at least a launchpad for sentencing.

Before presenting a sentencing protocol – the specific steps which may be taken by sentencers in an individual country, resulting in a certain "checklist" – in a proportional setting, I will briefly discuss whether such a protocol could also be designed for a system emphasising consequentialist sentencing rationales. I think that this would indeed be possible, yet there would need to be an agreement on the importance of each consequentialist sentencing rationale

2 At least in systems in which a prison sentence can be imposed for every criminal offence (as is the case in the majority of European countries).

and its application for certain groups of offenders. For example, when should incapacitation be more important than rehabilitation, and what role should deterrence play? Given this hierarchy of sentences, one would need to outline factors that need to be considered to provide sufficient background for making a decision and factors determining choices taken by sentencers. Lastly, these factors would need to be grouped to form specific steps, the order of which would reflect the hierarchy of consequentialist aims. The three steps outlined in Chapter 3 (specification, importance and weighing) would also apply.

Seven sentencing steps: its application in Czechia

The sentencing protocol needs to reflect the specificity of the sentencing system in an individual country. Any detailed discussion of a sentencing process thus needs to be rooted within a specific system; abstract analysis would, in my opinion, complicate understanding of the concept. Therefore, I outline the sentencing process as it would be suitable for the Czech criminal justice system – given that this book focuses on post-communist countries, the Czech system is rather typical of them, and I am the most familiar with this system – while also discussing deviations which may be appropriate for other (different) systems. In designing the sentencing protocol, I have taken inspiration especially from English sentencing guidelines, improving them by emphasising the concept of a penal value (taken from the Swedish penal system) and providing a structure that would guide judges to make specific decisions and include reasons for them.

I first briefly outline the Czech sentencing system to enable readers to understand it. Czech judges are given broad discretion regarding the imposition of both sentence type and length. The Czech penal code sets rather broad sentencing ranges for individual offences and outlines general principles of sentencing. It defines the very basic principles of sentencing multiple offenders, provides lists of mitigating and aggravating factors and directs judges to consider a wide array of factors. There are no sentencing guidelines and sentence orientations (starting points). There is no sentencing rationale as it was purposefully not included, even though the proportionality requirement is mentioned in the penal code and emphasised by the Constitutional Court, which in effect adopted a limiting retributivist approach.[3]

Limiting retributivism is also my guiding principle in constructing a sentencing process. The first step thus needs to set a penal value for the sanctioned behaviour, specifically determining the length of a provisional prison sentence that could not be exceeded in the following steps. Next, judges should consider factors not relating to the offence's seriousness, including previous

3 Decision n. I. ÚS 4503/12 made on 11. 6. 2014 (N 119/73 Sb. U 827), point 26, accessible at nalus.usoud.cz. Such an approach was, however, not fully embraced by lower courts and was not fully followed by the Constitutional Court in other decisions (even implicitly).

convictions. As a result, a provisional prison sentence would either decrease or remain the same. A decision on whether to incarcerate the offender or not is the next step; given that incarceration is considered an exceptional measure in Czechia, there are only a few selected reasons for its imposition. Then, signals of procedural cooperation – especially guilty pleas – are considered. Sentence imposition ensues with, first, the consideration of offenders' risks and needs – resulting in the imposition of rehabilitative or incapacitative sentences and measures – and, if an offender is not incarcerated, the selection of an appropriate intermediate sanction the length of which would reflect the penal value of the sanctioned behaviour and the penal bite of other sanctions and measures. As a final correction, multiple convictions would be considered, so that a judge would not impose a detrimental sentence.

Individual steps, their number and what judges consider within them first reflect proportionality as a guiding principle by setting a penal value and considering other factors not related to an offences' seriousness (and by considering procedural cooperation after the decision on incarceration is made). Other steps and their order were primarily determined by practical concerns; given that the choice of rehabilitative measures will depend on whether an offender is incarcerated or not, the decision on incarceration precedes the setting of rehabilitative and incapacitative measures. As these measures have a punitive bite, they also precede the decision on the non-custodial sanction type. Consideration of multiple convictions is the last correction. I do not claim that such a process is the only one possible or that it is perfect, but only that it reflects proportionality, practical concerns and the Czech context.

Such a sentencing process would not only guide judges in imposing sentences but also provide them with an opportunity to present reproducible and understandable sentence justification. Such justification could be taken using a form outlining the steps mentioned in a previous paragraph and displayed in Figure 7.1. Groups of factors that need to be considered within the Czech system are divided into individual steps when they should be considered. Their direction and importance can be easily recorded in the form, and judges are directed to weigh all factors in each step to arrive at a specific conclusion. The final sentence is then the result of consideration of all the steps.

I next discuss each step in greater detail. In each of the individual steps, I insert factors that need to be considered according to the Czech Penal Code and I consider carrying out the three stages of reasoning – specification, direction and importance and weighing. Following all seven steps would lead judges to arrive at a final sentence. Such a sentencing process would not only guide judges to impose sentences in a principled way but would also provide them with an opportunity to present a reproducible and understandable justification of an imposed sentence.

1. Penal value proportionate to offense seriousness	Strength
Degree of culpability	– ●●•∅∘○○ +
Motive/goal	– ●●•∅∘○○ +
Harm	– ●●•∅∘○○ +
Consequences for the victim and society	– ●●•∅∘○○ +
Context within which it was committed	– ●●•∅∘○○ +
Provisional prison sentence	DAYS .... MONTHS

Figure 7.1 Sentencing protocol – penal value

Step 1: Specifying a penal value proportionate to offence seriousness

First, judges need to specify the penal value of the behaviour: a provisional prison sentence proportionate to the seriousness of the offences. This sentence sets the maximum sentence that could be imposed, no matter how the offender behaves after he or she has committed the offences or how repulsive they might seem. Seriousness is determined by both the offender's culpability (its degree and motive/goal) and harm, including the consequences for the victim and society. Specific aspects relating to only some groups of offenders, such as the extent of contribution of any accomplices, the significance and nature of their involvement for participants in cases with multiple offenders, would be considered, as well as multiple offending. A complex perspective of offence seriousness would be provided by examining the context in which the offence was committed.

The first step can be expressed as in Figure 7.1; this provides an option to specify these factors to make their manifestation in the discussed case explicit. Then, the judge needs to make an approximate judgment about whether the factor aggravates (-) or mitigates (+) and its approximate strength (low, medium or high). This enables the judge to weigh all the factors together more easily in order to arrive at a provisional prison sentence of a specific length. To do so, consideration of a sentencing range theory – where an average offence within a sentencing range should be[4] – applicable in the individual system needs to take place. Ordinal proportionality would thus be achieved.

4 This position will differ, for example, according to whether the sentencing range already accounts for multiple offences to be imposed within the sentencing range or not.

2. Consideration of factors unrelated to offense seriousness	Strength
Previous convictions	∅ ∘ ○ ◯ +
Circumstances (personal, income, family, other)	∅ ∘ ○ ◯ +
Social context	∅ ∘ ○ ◯ +
Behavior after the act	∅ ∘ ○ ◯ +
Expected effects of conviction on the offender	∅ ∘ ○ ◯ +
Criminal proceedings (length)	∅ ∘ ○ ◯ +
Adjusted provisional prison sentence	.... Days Months

Figure 7.2 Sentencing protocol – mitigating factors

While such an approach might resemble the "quantification" of a sentencing process, it is only a formal expression of what the judge's daily bread is: comparing the seriousness of a particular behaviour with the seriousness of other behaviours which people commit and imposing a sentence accordingly. Nevertheless, Czech judges would need to change their approach to sentencing. Specifically, they would have to abandon the concept of "what sentences are imposed at this court" and adopt a limiting retributivist perspective that first sets proportionate sentences and only then reduces them for additional reasons.

Sentence orientations could be especially helpful to situate a specific behaviour among others and to quantify its penal value. Specifically, for frequently occurring offences, multiple starting points outlying basic behavioural scenarios could be defined and anchored on the applicable sentencing range. When coupled with an outline of approximately how a specific factor's presence should influence seriousness consideration, a starting point of consistent and principled sentencing might appear.

Step 2: Factors unrelated to offence seriousness

In the second step – displayed in Figure 7.2 – judges will specify and consider factors unrelated to offence seriousness. Limiting retributivism dictates that these factors could only lead to the reduction of a provisional prison sentence, allowing factors to have either no or positive direction of different strengths. These factors, when weighed together, would result in an adjusted prison sentence. Three groups of factors to be considered at this step are previous convictions, offender circumstances and those relating to criminal proceedings.

Prior convictions do not directly relate to offence seriousness; harm is not greater when an offence was committed by a first-time offender than by a repeat offender, and offenders' culpability towards the specific behaviour does not significantly change either. However, previous convictions are universally viewed as a factor that has to be considered even by many proportionalists (Frase & Roberts, 2019, Chapter 1; Roberts & von Hirsch, 2010). Here, I employ a theoretical concept of first offender "advantage," which the offender gradually loses (the so-called "progressive loss of mitigation" approach (Frase & Roberts, 2019, pp. 28–33; Roberts, 2010; Von Hirsch, 2010)). On this approach, there would be no increase – but also no discount – for a repeat offender, while a first-time offender's provisional prison sentence would be lowered.[5]

Second, offender circumstances would be considered, as they do not relate to offence seriousness. Yet only circumstances that do not relate directly to the offender's culpability would be considered; those influencing culpability towards the sanctioned behaviour would be considered in Step 1. The circumstances considered in Step 2 could range from the offender's age and the way in which he or she was brought up to their role in a society or family situation. At this point, I am not making a judgment call about what factors should result in lowering a prison sentence, but I am simply repeating factors mentioned by the Czech Penal Code. The specification of a factor should lead judges not to consider the same element twice.

Lastly, various other factors relating to criminal proceedings should be considered at this point. The offender's behaviour after the act, such as expressing remorse and reparation of damages, does not reduce offence seriousness, yet it does fulfil other sentencing aims, namely restorative justice (note that a guilty plea is considered in Step 4). Overly long criminal proceedings should also result in a reduced sentence, which is a requirement of the European Court of Human Rights. Lastly, the conviction's effect on the offender's employment or public discussion of the case could be considered at this point.

Consideration of all these factors would result in an adjusted prison sentence. The process would thus reveal what factors contributed to the adjustment of a provisional prison sentence and approximately in what way. Quantifying the penal value to reflect the offender's behaviour and person would allow the court to make the first decision on what sentence should be imposed.

Step 3: Decision on incarceration

A decision on whether to incarcerate an offender would be next, as other choices – such as whether and what rehabilitative or incapacitative measures to impose – depend upon whether the offender will remain in the community

5 Other approaches to previous convictions which suggest that an offender's previous convictions increase their culpability would ned to be considered in the first step as the "offender's general culpability," in contrast to culpability relating to the committed behaviour.

or not. Different countries evaluate the conditions for imprisonment differently. In some countries – such as in Czechia – a non-suspended prison sentence is considered a sanction of a last resort; in others, a non-suspended prison sentence is just one of several options. Some systems consider a suspended prison sentence to be a prison sentence, whereas others do not (such as Czechia in practice (Drápal, 2021)). In some countries, a prison sentence can be transformed into a different sanction after it has been imposed, while in others it is impossible. Some allow (only) seriousness and previous convictions to influence this behaviour, whereas others – such as Sweden – have a special category of offences for which a non-suspended prison sentence should be imposed even if both the seriousness and the number of previous convictions are low. Conditions for incarcerating an offender set out in this step will thus be strongly context-dependent.

In Czechia, there are two primary reasons to incarcerate an offender: offence seriousness and re-offending risk. The seriousness is easy to establish, since a provisional prison sentence was determined in a previous step. An approximate threshold could thus be defined. In Sweden, such a threshold (zone) is set at around one year of imprisonment (Jareborg & Žíla, 2022, Chapter 14.4.3). The specific value within each country would in many respects depend upon how high the sentencing range minimums are and the threshold and criteria for suspension of a prison sentence. In Czechia, the threshold could be placed around a provisional sentence of 36 months, which corresponds to the possibility of suspending a prison sentence; an offence's seriousness should not be considered when deciding on suspension (Drápal, 2022b).[6] This threshold is rather high, yet it reflects high sentencing-range minimums.

The second reason is a high risk of re-offending, which is typically largely based on the offender's previous convictions. The rationale for this is to protect society by incapacitating the offender. In the Czech Republic, a prison sentence is previewed as a sanction of last resort; its imposition thus needs to be considered as a necessity, and it might also be viewed as a failure of the system's previous attempts. As with offence seriousness, it might be helpful to approximately define the threshold, for example by using risk-assessment tools. Yet as of 2024, none is used in Czechia. I therefore do not discuss this custodial threshold (zone) in detail.

Additionally, less common reasons for which it would be practical to incarcerate an offender might appear. For example, if an offender commits an offence by not starting to serve a prison sentence when ordered (a frequent offence in Czechia), imposing a different sentence than a prison sentence would be impractical. Similarly, when imposing a sentence on an offender who is serving a long prison sentence, a prison sentence is likely the only

6 Similarly, for offences with sentencing range maximums of up to 5 years, seriousness should not play a (decisive) role when deciding whether to imprison an offender (s. 55/2).

3. Decision on incarceration	Incarceration
Seriousness	Yes | No
	OR
Re-offending risk	Yes | No
	OR
Other reason for incarceration	Yes | No
	AND
Is there a reason that trumps the decision to incarcerate (eg parent of a minor)?	No | Yes
Incarceration	Yes | No

Figure 7.3 Sentencing protocol – custodial threshold

possible solution even for an offence of low seriousness (such as using narcotics in a prison). However, such reasons should be limited and used with caution, following the approach of the Czech system to incarceration.

Finally, even if there is a reason to incarcerate an offender, this might be trumped by exceptional factors, such that incarceration is deemed an inappropriate solution. The Czech Constitutional Court has thus discussed at length conditions in which an offender who is the parent of a child should not be incarcerated, even though imprisonment would otherwise be warranted. Offence seriousness could thus be – to a certain degree – outweighed by the fact that an offender is a single parent caring for a small child.[7] Such an approach would, however, likely be rather exceptional.

When deciding whether to imprison an offender or not in the third step, the checks displayed in Figure 7.3 could help to determine the outcome: has a serious offence been committed? Is there a high risk of re-offending? Is there another reason, or does another factor trump these reasons, so that the offender should not be incarcerated? These clearly defined rules might emphasise system preferences; a judge might think that a combination of a mid-serious offence and a mid-level risk should result in incarceration, while the criteria might direct him or her towards non-incarceration. As a result, both the decision whether to imprison an offender or not and the reasons for it should be made clearer.

Step 4: Procedural cooperation

Criminal investigations and proceedings require an important investment of resources from criminal justice systems. Naturally, criminal justice systems also try to limit their expenses by providing incentives to defendants to cooperate with the aim of shortening the proceedings. Such cooperation might consist of different types of guilty pleas, plea bargaining or designating relevant facts

7 Decision n. IV. ÚS 950/19 made on 14. 4. 2020 (N 70/99 SbNU 362), points 54–56, available at nalus.usoud.cz.

4. PROCEDURAL COOPERATION	DISCOUNT AMOUNT
Guilty plea	
Adjusted provisional prison sentence	DAYS .... MONTHS

Figure 7.4 Sentencing protocol – procedural cooperation

as undisputed (all these options are a possibility in Czechia). These factors are distinct from the offender's behaviour after the act at Step 2, which reflects the offender's attitude towards the victim and society; especially restorative aims are sought. In contrast to these, the primary purpose of procedural cooperation is system effectiveness. The different principles sought justify why behaviour after the act might result in non-incarceration (and is thus considered at Step 2), while procedural cooperation cannot, and is thus considered at Step 4.

The main reasons for incarcerating an offender expressed in Step 3 are twofold: offence seriousness and re-offending risk. The proportionality principle dictates that, if an offender has committed a crime of such severity that only a non-suspended prison sentence has sufficiently high penal bite to respond to its penal value, then the offender must be incarcerated unless in the event of exceptional circumstances (Roberts & Dagan, 2023; Roberts & Harris, 2017). Otherwise, a system would be more preoccupied with its effectiveness than proportionality (and justice). Similarly, if re-offending risk is so high that incarceration is the only option to prevent the offender from re-offending, it would be unsafe not to incarcerate him/her in exchange for procedural cooperation. Other solutions might be proposed either in exceptional circumstances or if a criminal justice system would otherwise collapse. In the former case, a certain preference of the system's effectiveness over proportionality should be, however, made official.

Consideration of procedural cooperation – expressed primarily through guilty pleas – should thus primarily influence the extent of the sentence by an adjustment of a provisional prison sentence, as is suggested in Figure 7.4. As a result, either a shorter prison term or shorter intermediate sanctions will be imposed; it would also be imaginable to impose an intermediate sanction according to the offender's preferences. The extent and quality of procedural cooperation should, however, be specified, and its importance should be clearly expressed so that it can be understood why a specific amount of discount was provided.

Step 5: Rehabilitative and incapacitative sentences/measures

Limiting retributivism emphasises that proportionality is not the only sentencing aim which should be pursued. Judges need to be directed to think about offenders' risks and needs and about sanctions' penal bite, as rehabilitative and incapacitative sentences and measures limit offenders in the way they lead their lives. Figure 7.5 emphasises both these aspects following the Czech Code of Criminal process; factors leading to the offences and enabling them are among the six categories of facts for which evidence needs to be gathered (s. 89/1). Once these are identified, judges may decide which rehabilitative and incapacitative sentences and measures need to be imposed. The need to specify risks and needs might contribute to judges not omitting the imposition of the required rehabilitative and incapacitative sentences and measures.

Rehabilitative and incapacitative sanctions and measures influence offenders' lives; therefore a provisional prison sentence should be adjusted to consider the penal bite. A ban on frequenting football games or a driving ban, a requirement to undergo work-related training or not to drink alcohol or probationary supervision are examples of such limitations. However, not all such sentences or measures should be considered (or alternatively their penal bite could be low); for example, a confiscation of tools used to commit an offence would have no or very low penal bite. The provisional prison sentence should be shortened to reflect the penal bite of rehabilitative and incapacitative sanctions and measures, unless it is possible to consider the extent of their execution following a breach resulting in imprisonment (which is often complicated, see Drápal (2022c)). Following the deduction of this penal bite, the final adjusted provisional prison sentence is defined.

This step shows a small deficiency of the suggested decision tree model; various rehabilitative and incapacitative measures might be considered suitable given the choice of a non-custodial sanction type in the next step. The implementation of the fifth and sixth steps should thus be carried out in coordination with each other. Rehabilitative and incapacitative sentences and measures are mentioned first for two reasons. First, their penal bite needs to be considered when deciding on the length of main sanctions, and so this needs to be set prior to the decision on the main sanction. Additionally, the law limits the imposition of some rehabilitative and incapacitative sentences or measures alongside only certain main sanctions; for instance, it is impossible

5. Rehabilitative and incapacitative sentences/measures

Factors leading to the offense		
Factors enabling the offense		
Incapacitative sanctions/measures needed to be imposed:	Penal bite	.... DAYS MONTHS
Rehabilitative sanctions/measures needed to be imposed:	Penal bite	.... DAYS MONTHS
Final adjusted provisional prison sentence		.... DAYS MONTHS

Figure 7.5 Sentencing protocol – rehabilitative and incapacitative measures

6. DECISION ON A MAIN SANCTION (ONLY IF OFFENDER IS NOT INCARCERATED AT [STEP 3])

What main sanction can be imposed	Fine	Community service	Susp. prison sentence	House arrest
Should it be imposed and why?				
1 MONTH OF PRISON SENTENCE =	15	30 hours	1 month	1 month
AMOUNT	... DF +	.... hours +	.... months +	.... months

Figure 7.6 Sentencing protocol – choice of alternative sanctions

to impose a supervision alongside a fine. If offenders' risks and needs warrant the imposition of certain rehabilitative and incapacitative sentences or measures, they should be imposed, and the main non-custodial sanction type should be adjusted to it. The decision on rehabilitative and incapacitative sentences and measures therefore needs to precede the decision on a main non-custodial sanction, although both decisions need to be coordinated.

Step 6: Decision on a main non-custodial sanction

If a judge decides to incarcerate an offender at Step 3, no additional discussion about what sentence should be imposed is needed; in this scenario, a non-suspended prison sentence is imposed, and its length corresponds to the final adjusted provisional prison sentence. Otherwise, Czech judges typically decide between imposing a fine (in the form of a day-fine), community service, suspended prison sentence and house arrest (or a combination of all of these, with certain combinations being forbidden). Two decisions need to be made: what sentences are possible and appropriate and their length.

First, an explanation should be provided regarding what sentence types were chosen. This decision can be broken down into two sub-decisions: whether a sentence might be imposed and whether it should be imposed. Figure 7.6 thus first provides a tick-box suggesting whether a sentence might be imposed or not; this decision should reflect both "hard" rules (e.g., whether a sentence can be imposed following a sentencing range maximum) and "soft" rules, such as not fining a person without any means. If multiple sentence types are possible, the appropriate one needs to be chosen; space is provided for judges to explain why the sentence was an appropriate one. We can imagine that proportionality concerns direct judges (not) to impose a certain main sanction type, but we do not elaborate on it at this point as the Czech Penal Code does not discuss it at a high level of detail.

Second, the length of intermediate sentences – which should reflect the length of the final provisional prison sentence – needs to be determined. To do this, a sanction's commensurability, a principle discussed at the beginning of this chapter, is required. In Figure 7.6, I employ the ratios outlined by the Czech Penal Code following breaches or defaults. Using these conversion rates, judges can easily determine an exact amount of intermediate sanctions. This thought process does not require any reasoning; it is straightforward and does not consist in any discretionary decision being taken.[8]

Step 7: Multiple convictions

The final possible adjustment of the sentence relates to multiple conviction cases. Prior to the current sentencing, a sentence has already been imposed on these offenders, which, however, has not yet been executed and which offenders will have to continue serving after the imposition of the new sentence. This issue is so specific and complicated (Drápal, 2023b) that its inclusion in one of the previous steps would distort the sentencing process. Its position at the very end reflects both its specificity and the Czech Penal Code, which states that a sentence should be imposed in such a way that, when coupled with so-far unserved sentences, it should not result in a disproportionate sentence. Any correcting mechanism should be present at the end of a process.

Complete sentencing protocol

All seven steps are combined in Figure 7.7. If this is adhered to by the judges, it will first guide them through the process of sentence imposition. Especially novice judges could strongly benefit from the complex sentencing process being broken down into seven steps and being told what factors to consider and what type of decision to make at each step. Such a sentencing protocol also reflects sentencing rationales and the extent to which some of them are preferred over others. Second, the sentencing protocol provides clear justification for every decision taken by judges; this enables stakeholders to understand why a sentence was imposed and to possibly review it.

The contribution of different criminal justice actors to a principled process

The structuring of a sentencing process should contribute to a proper application of sentencing principles that is understandable for different audiences, with a possible secondary aim of developing sentencing principles. To achieve these purposes, the sentencing process should be structured not only in relation to the imaginary sentence imposition (such as the seven steps outlined above) but also in relation to the contributions of participating actors. The

8 The exception being an operational period of a suspended prison sentence.

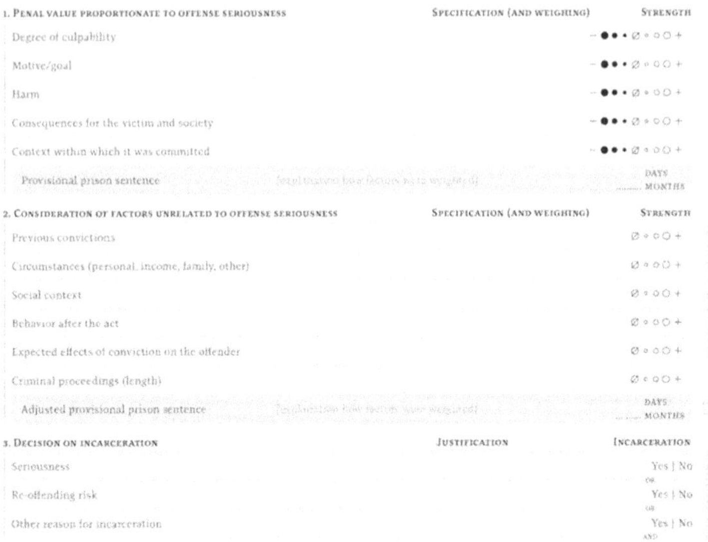

1. Penal value proportionate to offense seriousness	Specification (and weighing)	Strength
Degree of culpability		– ● ● • ∅ ∘ ○ ◯ +
Motive/goal		– ● ● • ∅ ∘ ○ ◯ +
Harm		– ● ● • ∅ ∘ ○ ◯ +
Consequences for the victim and society		– ● ● • ∅ ∘ ○ ◯ +
Context within which it was committed		– ● ● • ∅ ∘ ○ ◯ +
Provisional prison sentence	[explanation how factors were weighted]	……… days / months

2. Consideration of factors unrelated to offense seriousness	Specification (and weighing)	Strength
Previous convictions		∅ ∘ ○ ◯ +
Circumstances (personal, income, family, other)		∅ ∘ ○ ◯ +
Social context		∅ ∘ ○ ◯ +
Behavior after the act		∅ ∘ ○ ◯ +
Expected effects of conviction on the offender		∅ ∘ ○ ◯ +
Criminal proceedings (length)		∅ ∘ ○ ◯ +
Adjusted provisional prison sentence	[explanation how factors were weighted]	……… days / months

3. Decision on incarceration	Justification	Incarceration
Seriousness		Yes | No or
Re-offending risk		Yes | No or
Other reason for incarceration		Yes | No and

Figure 7.7 Sentencing protocol for Czechia – seven steps of a proper sentence justification

Note: I am very grateful to Michal Kuk for the graphical design of this forms and comments on it. Its Czech version has appeared in a journal *Státní zastupitelství* (Drápal, 2023a); the following ideas are discussed in greater detail there, and a few parts were directly translated from this article.

range of relevant actors will depend especially on whether prosecutors recommend a sentence in a specific system and to what extent appellate and supreme courts rule on sentences. I will briefly discuss the roles of different actors in Czechia, where prosecutors recommend sentences and appellate courts routinely review sentences (see Chapter 5), but the Supreme Court does not.

A powerful but sometimes hidden group of actors are prosecutors, whose recommendations strongly influence imposed sentences (Drápal & Dušek, 2023; Englich et al., 2006; Enough & Mussweiler, 2001). The recommended sentences should thus already be structured. The structuring of their decisions would further contribute to a proper sentencing discussion taking place in front of first-level courts; the evidence underlying the consideration of individual factors in which sentence recommendation is rooted would then be disclosed. Defendants might thus provide new evidence to counter the evidence suggested by prosecutors; judges – especially in systems with a stronger inquisitorial emphasis – might easily question the validity of the presented claims prior to deciding on a sentence. Possibly, defendants could file similar sentence

Is there a reason that trumps the decision to incarcerate (eg parent of a minor)? — AND No | Yes

Incarceration — Yes | No

4. PROCEDURAL COOPERATION — SPECIFICATION (AND WEIGHING) — DISCOUNT AMOUNT

Guilty plea

Adjusted provisional prison sentence — .... DAYS / MONTHS

5. REHABILITATIVE AND INCAPACITATIVE SENTENCES/MEASURES — SPECIFICATION (AND WEIGHING)

Factors leading to the offense

Factors enabling the offense

Incapacitative sanctions/measures needed to be imposed: — Penal bite .... DAYS / MONTHS

Rehabilitative sanctions/measures needed to be imposed: — Penal bite .... DAYS / MONTHS

Final adjusted provisional prison sentence — .... DAYS / MONTHS

6. DECISION ON A MAIN SANCTION (ONLY IF OFFENDER IS NOT INCARCERATED AT [STEP 3])

What main sanction can be imposed: Fine ☐ Community service ☐ Susp. prison sentence ☐ House arrest ☐

Should it be imposed and why?

1 MONTH OF PRISON SENTENCE =	15 day fines	30 hours	1 month	1 month
AMOUNT	.... DF +	.... hours +	.... months +	.... months

7. MULTIPLE CONVICTIONS — SENTENCE ADJUSTMENT

Unexecuted sentences the offender will have to execute.

Figure 7.7 (Continued)

recommendations on their own; such submission is imaginable even without seeing prosecutors' recommendations first, since it seems that if the defence is the last aspect considered in suggesting a sentence, it is to the defendant's disadvantage (Englich et al., 2005). If submissions by defendants were to become routine, it would be easier for them to not plead guilty, while at the same time having the possibility to influence a sentence in case they are found guilty.

Considering parties' submissions and clarifications during the main hearing, first-level courts might resolve contentious issues either prior to imposing a sentence or in their reasoning. Arguably, the portion of appeals might then decrease as parties would be persuaded by first-level courts' arguments. Appeals would thus only be filed following a disagreement on the consideration of either the evidence or the application of sentencing principles. Appellate and supreme courts would be provided with an opportunity to review clearly outlined principles, allowing them to elaborate and develop sentencing principles (as opposed to the current situation, see Chapter 5).

Conclusion

The justification of sentences as outlined in this chapter would enable stakeholders to better understand why a specific sentence was imposed than is possible in the current penal system. Offence seriousness would be clearly expressed, as both the penal value and reasons leading to the imposition of a more lenient sentence would be made explicit. There would be a comprehensible explanation as to why one of the most important decisions taken – whether to imprison an offender or not – was made and if intermediate sanctions were to be imposed, while the length of the sentence would understandably relate to offence seriousness. Similarly, offenders' risks and needs would be considered, and judges would show how these risks and needs were reflected in decisions they have taken. Overall, it would be easily understandable why judges made the decisions; if necessary, judges could simplify their thought process for specific audiences, such as the public. Justification: Done.

Prior to concluding, please allow me to address a few possible points of criticism, which also takes us back to the consideration in Chapter 2 concerning why judges should provide reasoning of high quality.

Would what is being proposed be too difficult for judges? I hope not, as judges should be doing all of these tasks at this point. The suggested approach does not place any additional burden on judges, but it simply requires them to do their job. A similar approach could be designed for criminal justice systems which employ complex sentencing guidance; this approach would ensure that all the factors and principles that should be taken into account are considered.

Would what is being proposed limit judges' discretion? No; it primarily structures the discretion but does not limit it. The only limitation is that, when structuring, some possibilities are not recommended (such as not incarcerating offenders following a guilty plea). It is a necessary consequence of adopting a limiting retributivism framework, which could be – with the same result – provided by an appellate or a Supreme Court when deciding on sentence proportionality and the role of a guilty plea.

Would it be too time-consuming? It might take judges longer to determine the sentence in this way and write it down. However, it should not be very long, likely not longer than half an hour. Given that sentencing is the most important decision for the offender[9] and is the most intrusive instrument a state has, half-hour considerations do not seem to be excessive. Similarly, if we consider the cost of a day in prison or the costs of probation, requiring a judge to spend half an hour to properly determine the amount of the sentence might be highly cost-effective. On the other hand, the provided sentencing protocol guides a judge through the process, making it easier for judges to impose sentences, compared with judges being lost in a myriad of factors. A slightly higher time demand might thus be offset by the attractiveness of a sentencing protocol.

Wouldn't it be impossible for judges to justify in detail the sentences they impose because sentencing principles are not sufficiently developed? This is

9 The decision on guilt has little or no consequence for the offender in itself.

the only criticism I would find valid, as it would be naturally difficult for judges to thoroughly justify decisions without being provided with a means to do so. Therefore, a short period during which sentencing scholarship summarises the most important findings and presents them to the judiciary – a requirement which is often lacking in post-communist Europe (Drápal & Plesničar, 2023) – might be provided. Yet no additional leeway should then be given; the details of the application of sentencing principles should be determined by the judicial system. The last thing to do is to persuade judges about the necessity of providing detailed justifications.

Would the sentencing protocol lead judges to impose sentences according to the provided steps? I hope that at least some judges will employ it in this way. However, other judges might go backwards, first by determining what sentence they want to impose and only then justifying the choices at each step. While it is important to be sceptical, the necessity to explain the choices made at individual steps might influence judges to at least alter their initial assessment if they discover that "it won't write," especially if appellate courts could review their assessment of individual steps. Yet one needs to be a healthy sceptic in this respect.

Since the 1970s, the structuring of sentencing discretion has been discussed by academics, and especially in the last few decades, important advances in the field of the role of individual sentencing principles have been made. I believe, however, that it is time to re-focus our attention upon the sentencing process, and in particular upon the application of these principles.[10] This book, and especially this chapter, suggest several ways in which the process of sentence imposition could be structured, improving both the principled nature of imposed sentences and their justification.

10 In this respect I am indebted to Mojca Plesničar; these matters arose to a large extent in discussions with her.

References

Abbink, H. (2016). Naar een model van strafmotivering. *Trema Straftoemetingsbulletin*, 14–18.

Arndt, J., Lieberman, J. D., Cook, A., & Solomon, S. (2005). Terror management in the courtroom: Exploring the effects of mortality salience on legal decision making. *Psychology, Public Policy, and Law*, *11*(3), 407–438. https://doi.org/10.1037/1076-8971.11.3.407

Ashworth, A. (2009). Techniques for reducing sentence disparity. In A. von Hirsch, A. Ashworth, & J. V. Roberts (Eds.), *Principled sentencing: Readings on theory and policy* (pp. 243–257). Hart Publishing.

Bartels, L. (2010). An examination of the arguments for and against the use of suspended sentences. *Flinders Law Journal*, *12*, 119–172.

Beaujean, R. G. A. (2008). Straffen is maatwerk, maar meten we wel met dezelfde maten? *Trema Straftoemetingsbulletin*, 20.

Beaujean, R. G. A. (2012). Van DCST naar een GIDS voor consistente straftoemeting? *Trema Straftoemetingsbulletin*, 15–22.

Beaujean, R. G. A. (2014). Voorlopig geen GIDS voor consistente straftoemeting. *Trema Straftoemetingsbulletin*, 3–9.

Berkowitz, M. C. (1974). The constitutional requirement for a written statement of reasons and facts in support of the sentencing decision: A due process proposal. *Iowa Law Review*, *60*(2), 205–238.

Bobek, M. (2010). O odůvodňování soudních rozhodnutí. *Právní Rozhledy*, *6*, 204–211.

Buber, M. (1970). *I and Thou*. Charles Scribner's Sons.

Burgess, H. (2017). A critical assessment of the duty of district court judges to given reasons. *Irish Judicial Studies Journal*, *1*, 49–55.

Burney, E. (1985). All things to all men: Justifying custody under the 1982 act. *Criminal Law Review*, *May*, 284–293.

Campbell, J. (1873). *The lives of the chiefJustices: Volume 3*. James Cockcroft & Co.

Cassidy, R. M., & Ullmann, R. L. (2016). Sentencing reform: The power of reasons. *Massachusetts Law Review*, *97*(4), 80–81.

Chanenson, S. L. (2006). Write on! *The Yale Law Journal Pocket Part*, *115*, 146–149.

Chater, N., & Oaksford, M. (2012). Normative Systems: Logic, Probability, and Rational Choice. In K. J. Holyoak & R. G. Morrison (Eds.), *The Oxford Handbook of Thinking and Reasoning* (pp. 11–21). Oxford University Press.

Chen, D. L. (2017). Implicit egoism in sentencing decisions: First letter name effects with randomly assigned defendants. *SSRN Electronic Journal*. https://doi.org/10.2139/ssrn.2928179

Claessen, J. A. A. C., & Meijer, S. (2022). Het project changing justice gears en de terugdringing van de korte gevangenisstraf. *Sancties*, *74*, 288–299.

Cohen, M. (2015). When judges have reasons not to give reasons: A comparative law approach. *Washington and Lee Law Review*, *72*(2), 483–501.

De Groot-van Leeuwen, L., Laemers, M., & Sportel, I. (2015). *Het vonnis beter uitgelegd? Maatschappelijke effecten van beter motiveren in de strafrechtspraak*. Raad voor de Rechtspraak Research Memoranda.

De Hullu, J. (2002). Enkele suggesties voor herziening van het strafrechtelijk sanctiestelsel. In J. de Hullu (Ed.), *Herziening van het sanctiestelsel; preadviezen voor de Nederlandse Juristen Vereniging* (pp. 1–87). Kluwer.

de Keijser, J. W., van Koppen, P. J., & Elffers, H. (2007). Bridging the gap between judges and the public? A multi-method study. *Journal of Experimental Criminology*, *3*(2), 131–161. https://doi.org/10.1007/s11292-007-9031-3

de Ridder, J et al. (2018), *Evaluatie Wet beperking oplegging taakstraf*, Pro Facto: Groningen.

Diamond, S. S., & Stalans, L. J. (1989). The myth of judicial leniency in sentencing. *Behavioral Sciences & the Law*, *7*(1), 73–89. https://doi.org/10.1002/bsl.2370070106

Dijkstra, A. J. C. (1998). *Vooronderzoek databank straftoemeting hoven met betrekking tot gevangenisstraffen van vier jaar of langer*. Ministerie van Justitie.

Drápal, J. (2018). Day fines: A European comparison and Czech malpractice. *European Journal of Criminology*, *15*(4). https://doi.org/10.1177/1477370817749178

Drápal, J. (2019). Odůvodnění trestů: Argumenty pro a proti detailnímu odůvodňování trestů. *Státní Zastupitelství*, 17(5), 15-24.

Drápal, J. (2020a). Odůvodnění trestů jako jediná manifestace diskrece při ukládání trestů: Nový přístup k tradičnímu institutu. In T. Gřivna & H. Šimánová (Eds.), *Ukládání trestů a jejich výkon*. Aleš Čeněk.

Drápal, J. (2020b). Odůvodnění trestů: Principy správného odůvodňování trestů. *Státní Zastupitelství*, 18(1), 8–17.

Drápal, J. (2021). Podmíněné odsouzení: Jeho účel a vývoj na území Česka. *Státní Zastupitelství*, *19*(6), 18–35.

Drápal, J. (2022a). Lze zohlednit závažnost při rozhodování o podmíněném odsouzení?. Mohou soudy zohledňovat závažnost trestného činu při rozhodování o podmíněném odložení výkonu trestu odnětí svobody? *Státní Zastupitelství*, *19*(6), 9–20.

Drápal, J. (2022b). Za reformu systému trestů: Citelnost trestů, jejich ekvivalence a nekoncepčnost současného systému. *Státní Zastupitelství*, *19*(2,3), 20–36, 8–17.

Drápal, J. (2023a). Jak strukturovaně ukládat a navrhovat tresty za zachování plné diskrece: Sedm fází ukládání trestů. *Státní Zastupitelství*, *20*(6), 16-28.

Drápal, J. (2023b). Sentencing multiple conviction offenders. *European Journal of Criminology*, *20*(1), 142–160. https://doi.org/10.1177/1477370821996903

Drápal, J., & Dušek, L. (2023). Law or authority: How penal elites shape dentencing policy by non-binding interventions. *SSRN Electronic Journal*. https://papers.ssrn.com/sol3/papers.cfm?abstract_id=4619030

Drápal, J., & Plesničar, M. (2023). Sentencing elsewhere: Structuring sentencing discretion in post-communist Europe. *European Journal on Criminal Policy and Research*. https://doi.org/10.1007/s10610-023-09568-4

Drápalová, J., & Drápal, J. (2022). Precedenční závaznost judikatury Ústavního soudu v praxi. *Bulletin Advokacie*, *7–8*, 33–45.

du Bois-Pedain, A., & Bottoms, A. E. (Eds.). (2019). *Penal censure: Engagements within and beyond desert theory*. Hart Publishing.

Duker, M. J. A. (2003). *Legitieme straftoemeting*. Boom Juridische uitgevers.

Elffers, H. (2016). *De straftoemetingsmal: Een middel om straftoemeting begrijpelijker te maken*. www.ivorentoga.nl/archieven/3983

Elffers, H. (2017). *De straftoemetingsmal in de gereedschapskist*. www.ivorentoga.nl/archieven/4227

Englich, B., Mussweiler, T., & Strack, F. (2005). The last word in court—A hidden disadvantage for the defense. *Law and Human Behavior*, *29*(6), 705–722. https://doi.org/10.1007/s10979-005-8380-7

Englich, B., Mussweiler, T., & Strack, F. (2006). Playing dice with criminal sentences: The influence of irrelevant anchors on experts' judicial decision making. *Personality and Social Psychology Bulletin*, *32*(2), 188–200. https://doi.org/10.1177/0146167205282152

Enough, B., & Mussweiler, T. (2001). Sentencing under uncertainty: Anchoring effects in the courtroom. *Journal of Applied Social Psychology*, *31*(7), 1535–1551. https://doi.org/10.1111/j.1559-1816.2001.tb02687.x

Ericsson, K. A. (2018). The differential influence of experience, practice, and deliberate practice on the development of superior individual performance of experts. In K. A. Ericsson, R. R. Hoffman, A. Kozbelt, & A. M. Williams (Eds.), *Cambridge handbook of expertise and expert performance* (pp. 745–769). Cambridge University Press.

Ernst, E. (2020). *Gelet op de aard en de ernst van het bewezenverklaarde. Een kwantitatief onderzoek naar de kwaliteit, begrijpelijkheid en acceptatie van straftoemeting* [Master thesis, Utrecht University]. https://www.njb.nl/blogs/begrip-en-acceptatie-van-strafvonnissen/

Evans, J. St. B. T. (2012). Dual-process theories of deductive reasoning: Facts and fallacies. In K. J. Holyoak & R. G. Morrison (Eds.), *The Oxford handbook of thinking and reasoning* (pp. 115–133). Oxford University Press.

Ewart, B. W., & Pennington, D. C. (1988). Reasons for sentence: An empirical investigation. *Criminal Law Review*, 584–599.

Feltovich, P. J., Prietula, M. J., & Ericsson, K. A. (2018). Studies of expertise from psychological perspectives: Historical foundations and recurrent themes. In K. A. Ericsson, R. R. Hoffman, A. Kozbelt, & A. M. Williams (Eds.), *Cambridge handbook of expertise and expert performance* (pp. 59–83). Cambridge University Press.

Ferrand, F. (2011). Odůvodnění soudních rozhodnutí v nauce a praxi—Francouzská zpráva. In L. Tichý, P. Holländer, & A. Bruns (Eds.), *Odůvodnění soudního rozhodnutí* (pp. 71–95). Univerzita Karlova v Praze.

Feteris, E. T. (2017). *Fundamentals of legal argumentation*. Springer Netherlands.

Fokkens, J. W. (2019). Enkele gedachten over straftoemeting en strafmotivering. In J. Balkema (Ed.), *Praktisch en veelzijdig (vriendenboek voor Paul Vegter)* (pp. 129–136). Kluwer.

Forman, P. (2023). *Odůvodňování trestů krajskými soudy* [Master thesis, Charles University, Faculty of Law]. http://hdl.handle.net/20.500.11956/186387

Frase, R. S. (2012). *Just sentencing*. Oxford University Press.

Frase, R. S., & Roberts, J. V. (2019). *Paying for the past*. Oxford University Press.

Freiberg, A. (2019). Suspended sentences in Australia: Uncertain, unstable, unpopular and unnecessary? *Law and Contemporary Problems*, *82*(1), 80–109.

Freiberg, A., & Sallmann, P. (2008). Courts of appeal and sentencing: Principles, policy and politics. *Law in Context*, *26*(1), 43–74. https://doi.org/10.3316/informit.231899681302588

Gertner, N. (2016). Opinions I should have written. *Northwestern University Law Review*, *110*(2), 423–438.

Goodman-Delahunty, J., & Sporer, S. L. (2010). Unconscious influences in sentencing decisions: A research review of psychological sources of disparity. *Australian Journal of Forensic Sciences*, *42*(1), 19–36. https://doi.org/10.1080/00450610903391440

Hall, M. A., & Wright, R. F. (2008). Systematic content analysis of judicial opinions. *California Law Review*, *96*(1), 63–122.

Hamilton, C. (2005). Sentencing in the district court: "Here be dragons." *Irish Criminal Law Journal*, *15*(3), 9–15.

Harris, L. (2022). *Achieving consistency in sentencing*. Oxford University Press.

Hassemer, R. (1983). Einige empirische Egebnisse zum Unterschied zwischen der Herstellung und der Darstellung richterlicher Sanktionenntscheidungen. *Monatsschrift Fur Kriminologie Und Strafrechtsreform*, *66*(1), 26–39.

Hessick, C. B. (2009). Appellate review of sentencing policy decisions after Kimbrough symposium: Criminal appeals: Sentencing appeals. *Marquette Law Review*, *93*(2), 717–750.

Hessick, C. B., & Hessick, F. A. (2008). Appellate review of sentencing decisions. *Alabama Law Review*, *60*(1), 1–40.

Hewton, T. (2010). Instinctive synthesis, structured reasoning, and punishment guidelines: Judicial discretion in the modern sentencing process. *Adelaide Law Review*, *31*, 79–93.

Ho, H. L. (2000). The judicial duty to give reasons. *Legal Studies*, *20*(1), 42–65.

Hogarth, J. (1971). *Sentencing as a human process*. University of Toronto Press.

Hosser, D., Windzio, M., & Greve, W. (2008). Guilt and shame as predictors of recidivism. *Criminal Justice and Behavior*, *35*(1), 138–152. https://doi.org/10.1177/0093854807309224

Hough, M., & Roberts, J. V. (1999). Sentencing trends in Britain. *Punishment & Society*, *1*(1), 11–26. https://doi.org/10.1177/14624749922227685

Hutton, N. (2006). Sentencing as a social practice. In S. Armstrong & L. McAra (Eds.), *Perspectives on punishment: The contours of control* (pp. 155–174). Oxford University Press.

Hutton, N. (2014). Sentencing as a cultural practice. In G. J. N. Bruinsma & D. Weisburd (Eds.), *Encyclopedia of criminology and criminal justice* (pp. 4724–4733). Springer.

Hutton, N. (2015). Visible and invisible sentencing. In A. Hondeghem, X. Rousseaux, & F. Schoenaers (Eds.), *Modernization of the criminal justice chain and the judicial system: New insights on trust, cooperation and human capital* (pp. 145–158). Springer.

Jacobson, J. (2013). *By mistakes we learn? A review of criminal appeals against sentence*. Tranform Justice. https://eprints.bbk.ac.uk/id/eprint/22242/1/transform-justice_appeals-report.pdf

Janssen, J. H., Kuster, P. H., & Paridaens, D. J. M. W. (2017). Belofte maakt schuld. *Trema Straftoemetingsbulletin, 1*, 12-16.

Jareborg, N. (1994). The Swedish sentencing law. *European Journal on Criminal Policy and Research, 2*(1), 67–83.

Jareborg, N., & Žila, J. (2022). *Straffrättens påföljdslära* (7th ed.). Författarna och Norstedts Juridik AB.

Killias, M. (1994). Sentencing reform—from rhetorics to reducing sentencing disparity. *European Journal on Criminal Policy and Research, 2*(1), 19–28.

King, R. D., & Johnson, B. D. (2016). A punishing look: Skin tone and afrocentric features in the halls of justice. *American Journal of Sociology, 122*(1), 90–124. https://doi.org/10.1086/686941

Kischel, U. (2011). Obsah soudního odůvodnění. In L. Tichý, P. Holländer, & A. Bruns (Eds.), *Odůvodnění soudního rozhodnutí* (pp. 399–413). Univerzita Karlova v Praze.

Klijn, A. (2017). *Het grote zwijgen van de ZM'*. www.ivorentoga.nl/archieven/4218

Kozinski, A. (1993). What I ate for breakfast and other mysteries of judicial decision making. *Loyola of Los Angeles Law Review, 26*(June), 993–999.

Krajewski, K. (2007). Too many suspended sentences? Polish or Central and Eastern European problem? *Sociologija. Mintis Ir Veiksmas, 2*, 109–121.

Krajewski, K. (2016). Sentencing in Poland: Failed attempts to reduce punitiveness. *Crime and Justice, 45*(1), 175–218.

Kremnitzer, M. (1991). Sentencing as art—a response: Sentencing as a just system. *Israel Law Review, 25*(3–4), 662–680.

Kuhn, A. (2002). Public and judicial attitudes to punishment in Switzerland. In J. V. Roberts & M. Hough (Eds.), *Changing attitudes to punishment: Public opinion, crime and justice* (pp. 115–127). Willan.

Labbe, R. M. (1977). Appellate review of sentences: Penology on the judicial doorstep criminology. *Journal of Criminal Law and Criminology, 68*(1), 122–134.

LeBoeuf, R., & Shafir, E. (2012). Decision making. In K. J. Holyoak & R. G. Morrison (Eds.), *The Oxford handbook of thinking and reasoning* (pp. 301–321). Oxford University Press.

Lensing, H. (2021). Oriëntatiepunten voor de straftoemeting. *Ars Aequi*, 541–556.

Lightowlers, C., Pina-Sánchez, J., & Watkins, E. D. (2022). Contextual culpability: How drinking and social context impact sentencing of violence. *Criminology & Criminal Justice, 22*(3), 442–461. https://doi.org/10.1177/1748895820972160

Liu, Z. (2018). Does reason writing reduce decision bias? Experimental evidence from judges in China. *Journal of Legal Studies, 47*, 83–118.

Lombrozo, T. (2012). Explanation and abductive inference. In K. J. Holyoak & R. G. Morrison (Eds.), *The Oxford handbook of thinking and reasoning* (pp. 260–276). Oxford University Press.

Marshall, P. D. (2011). A comparative analysis of the right to appeal. *Duke Journal of Comparative & International Law, 22*(1), 1–46.

Meijer, S., Laxminarayan, M., & de With, N. (2021). *Motivate. Een strafmotivering aan de hand van strafdoelen*. Vrije Universiteit Amsterdam.

Miller, M. (1989). Guidelines are not enough: The need for written sentencing opinions. *Behavioral Sciences and the Law, 7*(1), 3–24.

Ministry of Justice. (2020). *České soudnictví 2019: Výroční statistická zpráva.*

Molden, D. C., & Higgins, E. T. (2012). Motivated thinking. In K. J. Holyoak & R. G. Morrison (Eds.), *The Oxford handbook of thinking and reasoning* (pp. 390–409). Oxford University Press.

Monahan, J., & Skeem, J. L. (2016). Risk assessment in criminal sentencing. *Annual Review of Clinical Psychology, 12*(1), 489–513. https://doi.org/10.1146/annurev-clinpsy-021815-092945

Morris, N. (1977). Towards principled sentencing. *Maryland Law Review, 37*(2), 267–285.

Morris, N., & Tonry, M. (1990). *Between prison and probation: Intermediate punishments in a rational sentencing system*. Oxford University Press.

Mosier, K., Fischer, U., Hoffman, R. R., & Klein, G. (2018). Expert professional judgments and "naturalistic decision making." In K. A. Ericsson, R. R. Hoffman, A. Kozbelt, & A. M. Williams (Eds.), *Cambridge handbook of expertise and expert performance* (pp. 453–475). Cambridge University Press.

Mueller, G. O. W. (1961). Penology and appeal: Appellate review of legal but excessive sentences. *Vanderbilt Law Review, 15*(3), 671–698.

O'Malley, T. (2011). *Sentencing—towards a coherent system*. Round Hall.

OSCE. (2010). *Inadequate assessment of mitigating and aggravating circumstances by the courts*. Organization for Security and Co-operation in Europe Mission in Kosovo.

Pina-Sánchez, J., Gosling, J. P., Chung, H.-I., Bourgeois, E., Geneletti, S., & Marder, I. D. (2019). Have the England and Wales guidelines affected sentencing severity? An empirical analysis using a scale of severity and time-series analyses. *The British Journal of Criminology, 59*(4), 979–1001. https://doi.org/10.1093/bjc/azz005

Plesničar, M. M. (2013). The individualization of punishment: Sentencing in Slovenia. *European Journal of Criminology, 10*(4), 462–478. https://doi.org/10.1177/1477370812469858

Rawls, J. (1971). *A theory of justice*. Harvard University Press.

Roberts, J. V. (2010). First-offender sentencing discounts: Exploring the justifications. In J. V. Roberts & A. Von Hirsch (Eds.), *Previous convictions at sentencing* (pp. 17–36). Hart Publishing.

Roberts, J. V., & Dagan, N. (2023). Rewarding virtue: An ethical defence of plea-based sentence reductions. In J. V. Roberts & J. Ryberg (Eds.), *Sentencing the self-convicted the ethics of pleading guilty* (pp. 71–92). Hart Publishing.

Roberts, J. V., & Harris, L. (2017). Reconceptualising the custody threshold in England and Wales. *Criminal Law Forum, 28*(3), 477–499. https://doi.org/10.1007/s10609-017-9308-9

Roberts, J. V., & von Hirsch, A. (Eds.). (2010). *Previous convictions at sentencing*. Hart Publishing.

Robinson, P. H. (1994). Desert, crime control, disparity, and units of punishment. In A. Duff, S. Marshall, R. Dobash, & R. Dobash (Eds.), *Penal theory and practice: Tradition and innovation in criminal justice* (pp. 93–107). Manchester University Press.

Rosenbaum, B. L. (2013). Sentence appeals in England: Promoting consistent sentencing through Robust Appellate review. *Journal of Appellate Practice and Process, 14*(1), 81–158.

Ryberg, J., Roberts, J. V., & de Keijser, J. W. (Eds.). (2018). *Sentencing multiple crimes*. Oxford University Press.

Samuels, A. (1981). Giving reasons in the criminal justice and penal process. *The Journal of Criminal Law*, *45*(1), 51–58.

Schachar, Y. (1991). Sentencing as art. *Israel Law Review*, *25*(3–4), 638–661.

Schauer, F. (1995). Giving reasons. *Stanford Law Review*, *47*(April), 633–659.

Schiff, M. F. (1997). Gauging the intensity of criminal sanctions: Developing the Criminal Punishment Severity Scale (CPSS). *Criminal Justice Review*, *22*(2), 175–206.

Schoep, G. K. (2008). *Straftoemetingsrecht en strafvorming*. Kluwer.

Schoep, G. K., & Schuyt, P. M. (2005). *Instrumenten ter ondersteuning van de rechter bij de straftoemeting*. E.M. Meijers Instituut.

Schuyt, P. M. (2010). *Verantwoorde straftoemeting*. Kluwer.

Scott, R. W. (2013). The Skeptic's guide to Information sharing at sentencing. *Utah Law Review*, *1*, 345–408.

Sebba, L. (1978). Some explorations in the scaling of penalties. *Journal of Research in Crime and Delinquency*, *15*(2), 247–265. https://doi.org/10.1177/002242787801500209

Sebba, L., & Nathan, G. (1984). Further explorations in the scaling of penalties. *The British Journal of Criminology*, *24*(3), 221–249. https://doi.org/10.1093/oxfordjournals.bjc.a047451

Sentencing Council. (2019). *General guideline: Overarching principles – Sentencing*. https://www.sentencingcouncil.org.uk/overarching-guides/magistrates-court/item/general-guideline-overarching-principles/

Slawsky, T. D. (1990). The importance of statements of reasons in guideline sentencing. *Federal Sentencing Reporter*, *2*(8), 298–301.

Spellman, B. A., & Schauer, F. (2012). Legal reasoning. In K. J. Holyoak & R. G. Morrison (Eds.), *The Oxford handbook of thinking and reasoning* (pp. 719–735). Oxford University Press.

St Amand, M. D., & Zamble, E. (2001). Impact of information about sentencing decisions on public attitudes toward the criminal justice system. *Law and Human Behavior*, *25*(5), 515–528. https://doi.org/10.1023/A:1012844932754

Stewart, H. (2009). The trial judge's duty to give reasons for judgment in criminal cases. *Canadian Criminal Law Review*, *14*(1), 19–35.

Stürner, R. (2011). Účel řízení a odůvodnění soudního rozhodnutí. In L. Tichý, P. Holländer, & A. Bruns (Eds.), *Odůvodnění soudního rozhodnutí* (pp. 371–383). Univerzita Karlova v Praze.

Sweet, R. W., van Hook, D. E., & Di Lello, E. V. (1996). Towards a common law of sentencing: Developing judicial precedent in cyberspace. *Fordham Law Review*, *65*, 927–950.

Tak, P. J. (2001). Sentencing and punishment in The Netherlands. In M. Tonry & R. S. Frase (Eds.), *Sentencing and sanctions in Western Countries* (pp. 151–187). Oxford University Press.

Tangney, J. P., Stuewig, J., & Martinez, A. G. (2014). Two faces of shame: The roles of shame and guilt in predicting recidivism. *Psychological Science*, *25*(3), 799–805.

Tangney, J. P., Stuewig, J., Mashek, D., & Hastings, M. (2011). Assessing Jail Inmates' Proneness to shame and guilt. *Criminal Justice and Behavior*, *38*(7), 710–734. https://doi.org/10.1177/0093854811405762

Tata, C. (1997). Conceptions and representations of the sentencing decision process. *Journal of Law and Society*, *24*(3), 395–420.

Tata, C. (2002). Accountability for the sentencing decision process—towards a new understanding. In C. Tata & N. Hutton (Eds.), *Sentencing and society: International perspectives* (pp. 399–428). Ashgate.

Tata, C. (2007). Sentencing as craftwork and the binary epistomologies of the discretionary decission process. *Socio-Legal Studies*, *16*(3), 425–447.

Tata, C. (2019). "Ritual individualization": Creative genius at sentencing, mitigation, and conviction. *Journal of Law and Society*, *46*(1), 112–140. https://doi.org/10.1111/jols.12144

Tata, C. (2020). *Sentencing: A social process*. Palgrave Macmillan.

Thomas, D. A. (2003). Judicial discretion in sentencing. In L. Gelsthorpe & N. Padfield (Eds.), *Exercising discretion: Decision-making in the criminal justice system and beyond* (pp. 50–73). Willan Publishing.

Tyler, T. R. (1988). What is procedural justice? Criteria used by citizens to assess the fairness of legal procedures. *Law & Society Review*, *22*(1), 103–135.

Tyler, T. R. (2003). Procedural justice, legitimacy, and the effective rule of law. *Crime and Justice*, *30*, 283–357. https://doi.org/10.1086/652233

Tyler, T. R. (2007). Procedural justice and the courts. *Court Review*, *44*(2), 26–31.

Van den Hoven, P., & Plug, J. (2009). Wat Promis kan leren over de begrijpelijkheid van de rechtstaal. *Nederlands Juristenblad*, *84*, 1156–1160.

Van der Schaaf, J., & Malsch, M. (2015). Burgers over strafvonnissen. *Trema*, *38*(3) 96–102.

Vanča, T., & Drápal, J. (2023). Jak odvolací soudy rozhodují o odvoláních proti trestu? Empirická analýza rozhodnutí krajských soudů měnících výrok o trestu. *Trestní Právo*, *4*, 33an.

Von Hirsch, A. (2010). Proportionality and the progressive loss of mitigation: Some further reflections. In J. V. Roberts & A. von Hirsch (Eds.), *Previous convictions at sentencing* (pp. 1–16). Hart Publishing.

von Hirsch, A. (2017). *Deserved criminal sentences*. Hart Publishing.

von Hirsch, A., Ashworth, A., & Roberts, J. V. (Eds.). (2009). *Principled sentencing: Readings on theory and policy*. Hart Publishing.

von Hirsch, A., & Jareborg, N. (1991). Gauging criminal harm: A living-standard analysis. *Oxford Journal of Legal Studies*, *11*(1), 1–38.

Von Hirsch, A., Wasik, M., & Greene, J. (1989). Punishments in the community and the principles of desert. *Rutgers Law Journal*, *20*(3), 595–618.

Waits, K. (1983). Values, intuitions, and opinion writing: The judicial process and state court jurisdiction. *University of Illinois Law Review*, *4*, 917–975.

Weinberg, M. (2014). *Adequate, sufficient and excessive reasons*. http://classic.austlii.edu.au/au/journals/VicJSchol/2014/9.pdf

Wright, G., & Goodwin, P. (2008). Structuring the decision process: An evaluation of methods. In G. P. Hodgkinson & W. H. Starbuck (Eds.), *The Oxford handbook of organizational decision making* (p. 0). Oxford University Press. https://doi.org/10.1093/oxfordhb/9780199290468.003.0028

Index

For Product Safety Concerns and Information please contact our EU
representative GPSR@taylorandfrancis.com
Taylor & Francis Verlag GmbH, Kaufingerstraße 24, 80331 München, Germany

www.ingramcontent.com/pod-product-compliance
Ingram Content Group UK Ltd.
Pitfield, Milton Keynes, MK11 3LW, UK
UKHW022109190926
475702UK00013B/1339
9781032747446